Take It to Your Seat C

Reading & Language

2

Using the Centers

The centers in this book are intended for skill practice and reinforcement, not as an introduction to skills. It is important to model the use of each center before students are asked to do the tasks independently.

Why Use Centers?

- Centers are a motivating way for students to practice important skills.
- They appeal especially to kinesthetic and visual learners.
- The 12 centers in this book are self-contained and portable. Students can work at a desk, at a table, or on a rug.
- Once you've made the centers, they're ready to use at any time.

Before Using Centers

You and your students will enjoy using the centers more if you think through logistical considerations. Here are a few questions to resolve ahead of time:

- Will students select a center, or will you assign the centers and use them as a skill assessment tool?
- Will there be a specific block of time for centers, or will the centers be used throughout the day as students complete other work?
- Where will you place the centers for easy access by students?
- What procedure will students use when they need help with the center tasks?
- Will students use the answer key to check their own work?
- How will you use the center checklist to track student completion of the centers?

A Place for Centers

Make the centers ahead of time so that they are ready for student use whenever specific skill practice is indicated.

Store the prepared centers in a filing box or crate. If you wish the centers to be self-checking, include the answer key with the center materials.

Introducing the Centers

Use the student direction cover page to review the skill to be practiced.

Read each step to the students and model what to do, showing students the center pieces.

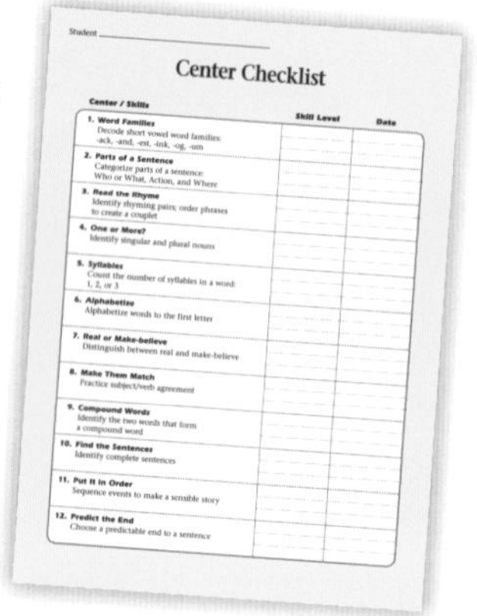

Record Progress

Use the center checklist (page 4) to record the date and student achievement.

Making the Centers

Included in Each Center

- (A) Student direction cover page
- (B) Task cards and/or mats
- (C) Reproducible student response form
- (D) Answer key

Materials Needed

- Colored file folders with inside pockets
- Small envelopes or plastic self-closing bags (for storing cut task cards)
- Pencils and marking pens (for labeling envelopes)
- Scissors
- Double-sided tape
- Laminated center pieces
- Answer key pages

Steps to Follow

1. Tape the student direction page to the front of the file folder.
2. Place the reproduced response forms in the left-hand pocket.
3. Laminate the task cards and mats. Put the cut cards in a labeled envelope or plastic self-closing bag. Place the mats and task cards in the right-hand pocket of the file folder.

A
B
C
D
Fantasy or Reality?
Fold answer key page in half as shown. Response form answers are on the back, and center answers are inside.
Assembled Center

Student ______________________________

Center Checklist

Center / Skills	Skill Level	Date
1. Rhyming Words Identify sets of rhyming words		
2. Make Words with Digraphs Form words beginning with consonant digraphs		
3. Listen for Long Vowels Distinguish the long vowel sound in words with several different spellings		
4. Alphabetical Order Alphabetize to the second letter		
5. Parts of a Sentence Categorize phrases as Who or What, Action, Where, or When		
6. More Than One Identify four ways (*s, es, ies,* and irregular) to make singular nouns plural		
7. Synonyms Identify words with similar meanings as synonyms		
8. Antonyms Identify words with opposite meanings as antonyms		
9. Homophones Identify the correct homophone to use in a sentence		
10. Fantasy or Reality? Distinguish whether a statement is based on fantasy or reality		
11. Sequencing Recognize that the events in a story follow a sequence		
12. Predict the Ending Choose a predictable ending to a sentence		

Take It to Your Seat Centers

Rhyming Words

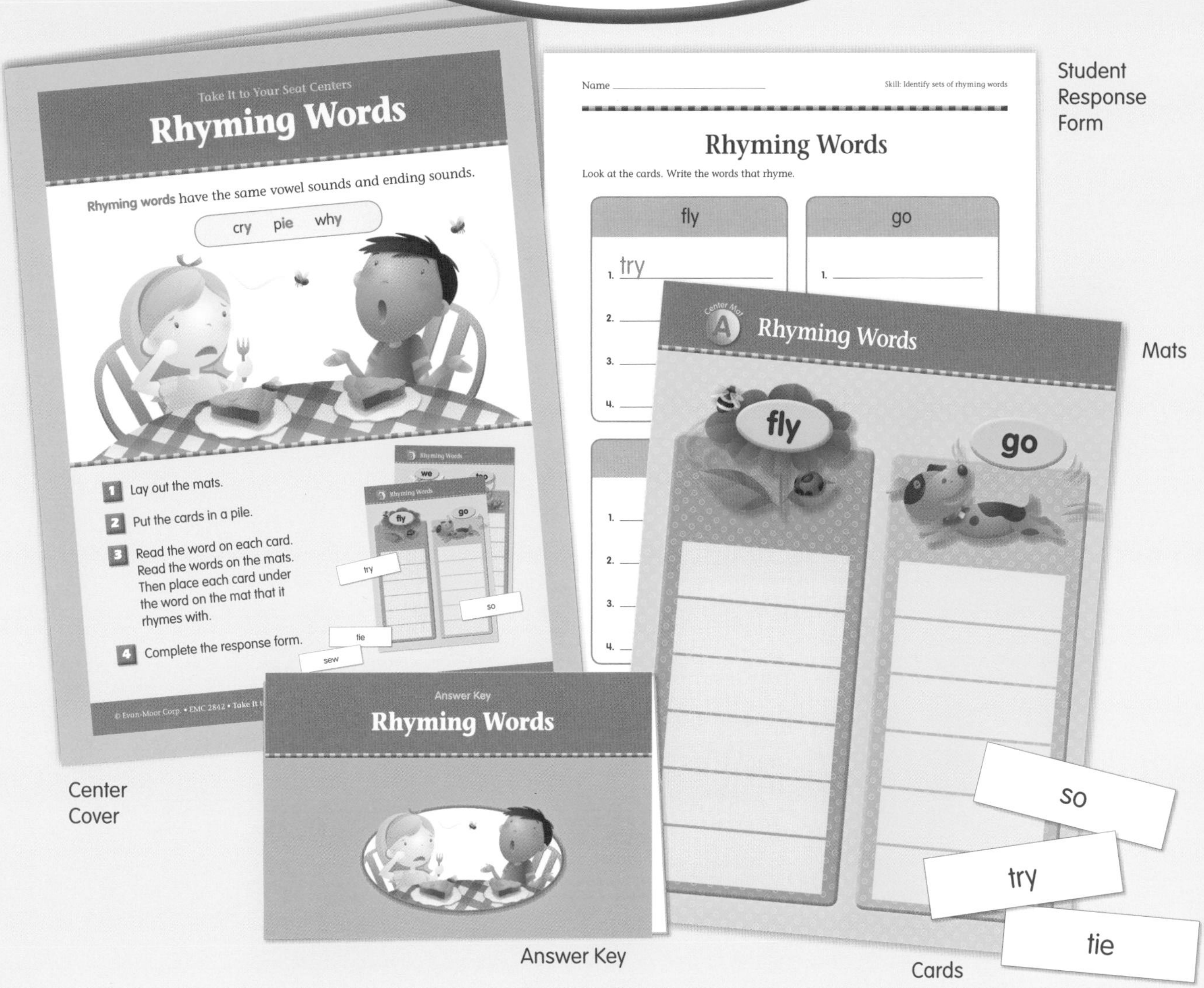

Student Response Form

Mats

Center Cover

Answer Key

Cards

Skill
Identify sets of rhyming words

Prepare the Center
Follow the directions on page 3.

Introduce the Center
Demonstrate how to use the center. State the goal: *You will decide if the word on each card rhymes with **fly**, **go**, **too**, or **we** and place it on the mat.*

Name ______________________ Skill: Identify sets of rhyming words

Rhyming Words

Look at the cards. Write the words that rhyme.

fly

1. try
2. ______
3. ______
4. ______

go

1. ______
2. ______
3. ______
4. ______

too

1. ______
2. ______
3. ______
4. ______

we

1. ______
2. ______
3. ______
4. ______

Rhyming Words

Rhyming words have the same vowel sounds and ending sounds.

cry pie why

1. Lay out the mats.
2. Put the cards in a pile.
3. Read the word on each card. Read the words on the mats. Then place each card under the word on the mat that it rhymes with.
4. Complete the response form.

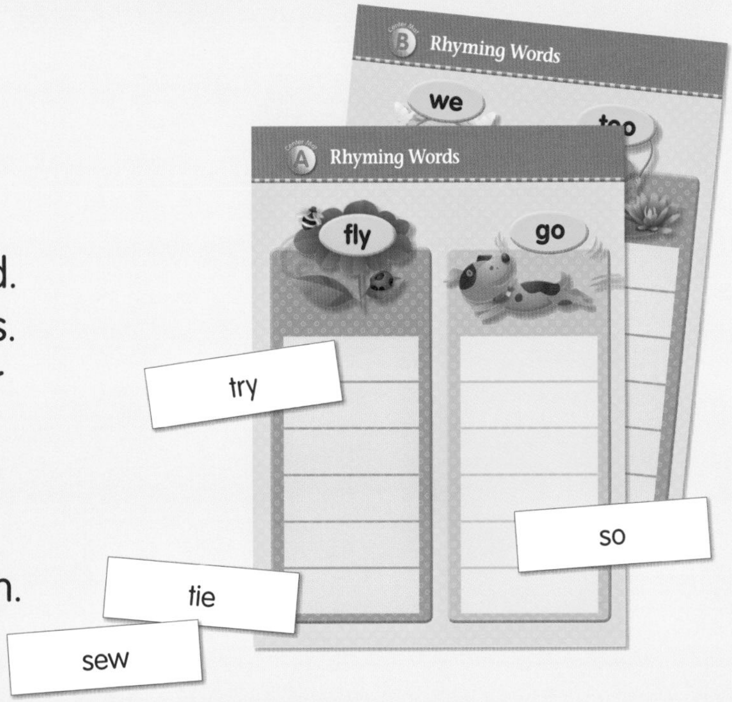

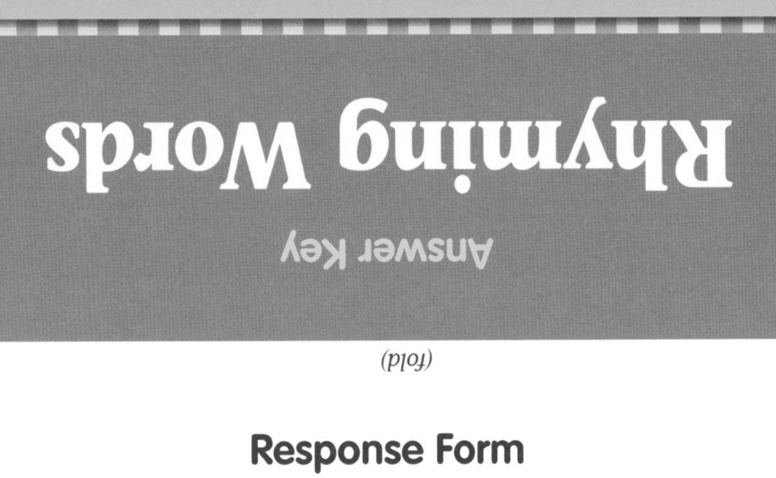

Answer Key

Rhyming Words

(fold)

Response Form

Rhyming Words

Look at the cards. Write the words that rhyme.

fly

1. try
2. tie
3. sky / pie
4. high / buy

go

1. so
2. sew
3. hoe / row
4. dough / blow

too

1. you
2. zoo
3. new / do
4. shoe / blue

we

1. bee
2. tree
3. flea / she
4. pea / sea

Answer Key

Rhyming Words

A

Center Mat A — Rhyming Words

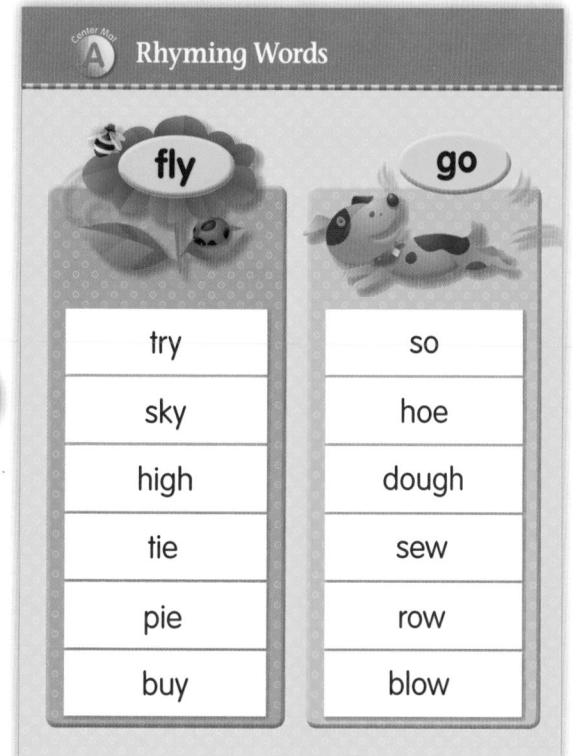

fly	go
try	so
sky	hoe
high	dough
tie	sew
pie	row
buy	blow

B

Center Mat B — Rhyming Words

we	too
bee	you
flea	new
pea	shoe
tree	zoo
she	do
sea	blue

Center Mat A

Rhyming Words

fly

go

Center Mat B

Rhyming Words

try	tie
sky	pie
high	buy
so	sew
hoe	row
dough	blow

Rhyming Words

Take It to Your Seat Centers
Reading & Language

Rhyming Words

Take It to Your Seat Centers
Reading & Language
EMC 2842 • © Evan-Moor Corp.

Rhyming Words

Take It to Your Seat Centers
Reading & Language
EMC 2842 • © Evan-Moor Corp.

Rhyming Words

Take It to Your Seat Centers
Reading & Language
EMC 2842 • © Evan-Moor Corp.

Rhyming Words

Take It to Your Seat Centers
Reading & Language
EMC 2842 • © Evan-Moor Corp.

Rhyming Words

Take It to Your Seat Centers
Reading & Language
EMC 2842 • © Evan-Moor Corp.

Rhyming Words

Take It to Your Seat Centers
Reading & Language
EMC 2842 • © Evan-Moor Corp.

Rhyming Words

Take It to Your Seat Centers
Reading & Language
EMC 2842 • © Evan-Moor Corp.

Rhyming Words

Take It to Your Seat Centers
Reading & Language
EMC 2842 • © Evan-Moor Corp.

Rhyming Words

Take It to Your Seat Centers
Reading & Language
EMC 2842 • © Evan-Moor Corp.

Rhyming Words

Take It to Your Seat Centers
Reading & Language
EMC 2842 • © Evan-Moor Corp.

Rhyming Words

Take It to Your Seat Centers
Reading & Language
EMC 2842 • © Evan-Moor Corp.

you	zoo
new	do
shoe	blue
bee	tree
flea	she
pea	sea

Rhyming Words

Take It to Your Seat Centers
Reading & Language
EMC 2842 • © Evan-Moor Corp.

Rhyming Words

Take It to Your Seat Centers
Reading & Language
EMC 2842 • © Evan-Moor Corp.

Rhyming Words

Take It to Your Seat Centers
Reading & Language
EMC 2842 • © Evan-Moor Corp.

Rhyming Words

Take It to Your Seat Centers
Reading & Language
EMC 2842 • © Evan-Moor Corp.

Rhyming Words

Take It to Your Seat Centers
Reading & Language
EMC 2842 • © Evan-Moor Corp.

Rhyming Words

Take It to Your Seat Centers
Reading & Language
EMC 2842 • © Evan-Moor Corp.

Rhyming Words

Take It to Your Seat Centers
Reading & Language
EMC 2842 • © Evan-Moor Corp.

Rhyming Words

Take It to Your Seat Centers
Reading & Language
EMC 2842 • © Evan-Moor Corp.

Rhyming Words

Take It to Your Seat Centers
Reading & Language
EMC 2842 • © Evan-Moor Corp.

Rhyming Words

Take It to Your Seat Centers
Reading & Language
EMC 2842 • © Evan-Moor Corp.

Rhyming Words

Take It to Your Seat Centers
Reading & Language
EMC 2842 • © Evan-Moor Corp.

Rhyming Words

Take It to Your Seat Centers
Reading & Language
EMC 2842 • © Evan-Moor Corp.

Make Words with Digraphs

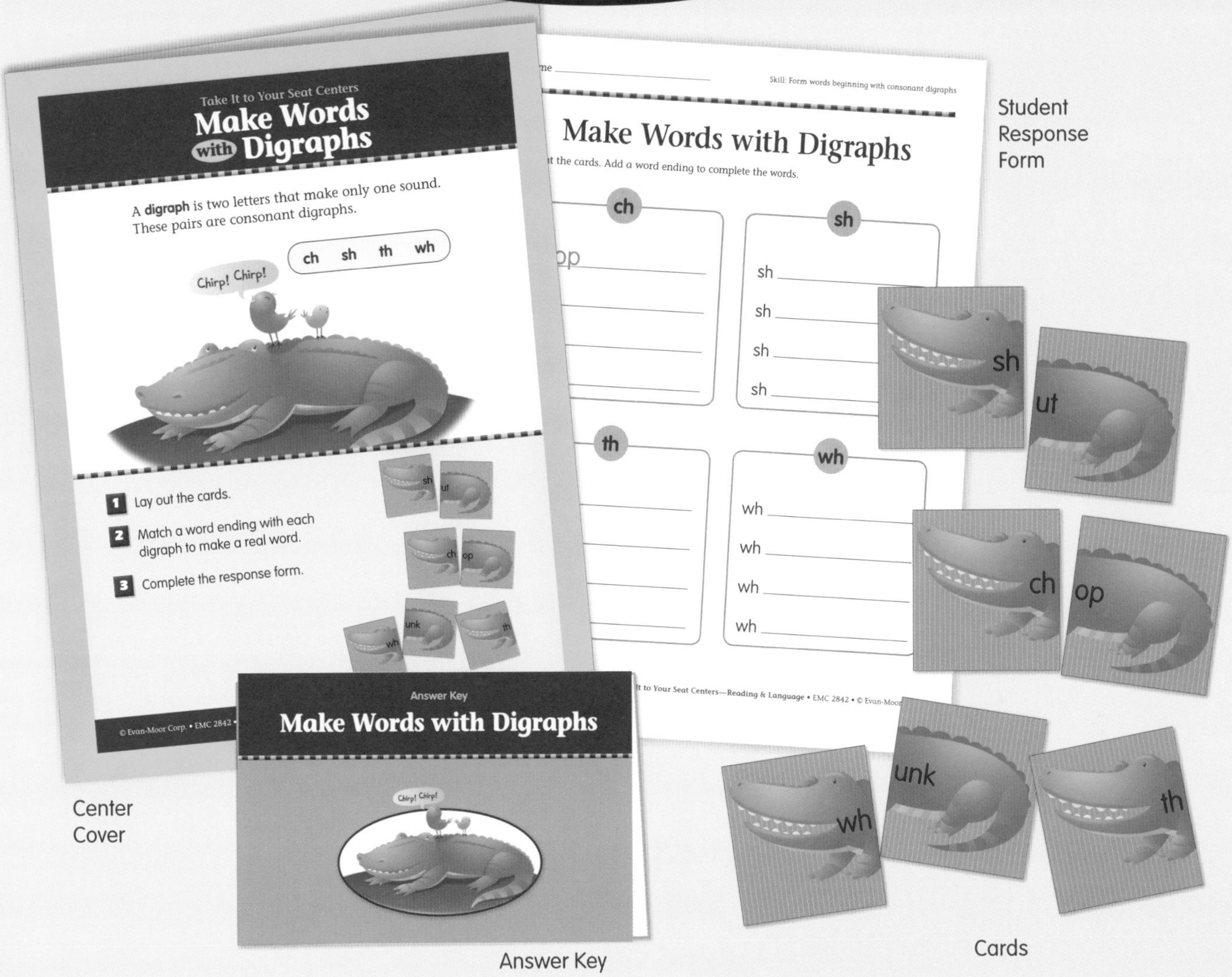

Skill
Form words beginning with consonant digraphs

Prepare the Center
Follow the directions on page 3.

Introduce the Center
Demonstrate how to use the center. State the goal: *You will add a word ending to each digraph to make 24 words.*

Name ______________________________ Skill: Form words beginning with consonant digraphs

Make Words with Digraphs

Look at the cards. Add a word ending to complete the words.

ch

ch op______________________

ch ______________________

ch ______________________

ch ______________________

sh

sh ______________________

sh ______________________

sh ______________________

sh ______________________

th

th ______________________

th ______________________

th ______________________

th ______________________

wh

wh ______________________

wh ______________________

wh ______________________

wh ______________________

Make Words with Digraphs

A **digraph** is two letters that make only one sound. These pairs are consonant digraphs.

ch sh th wh

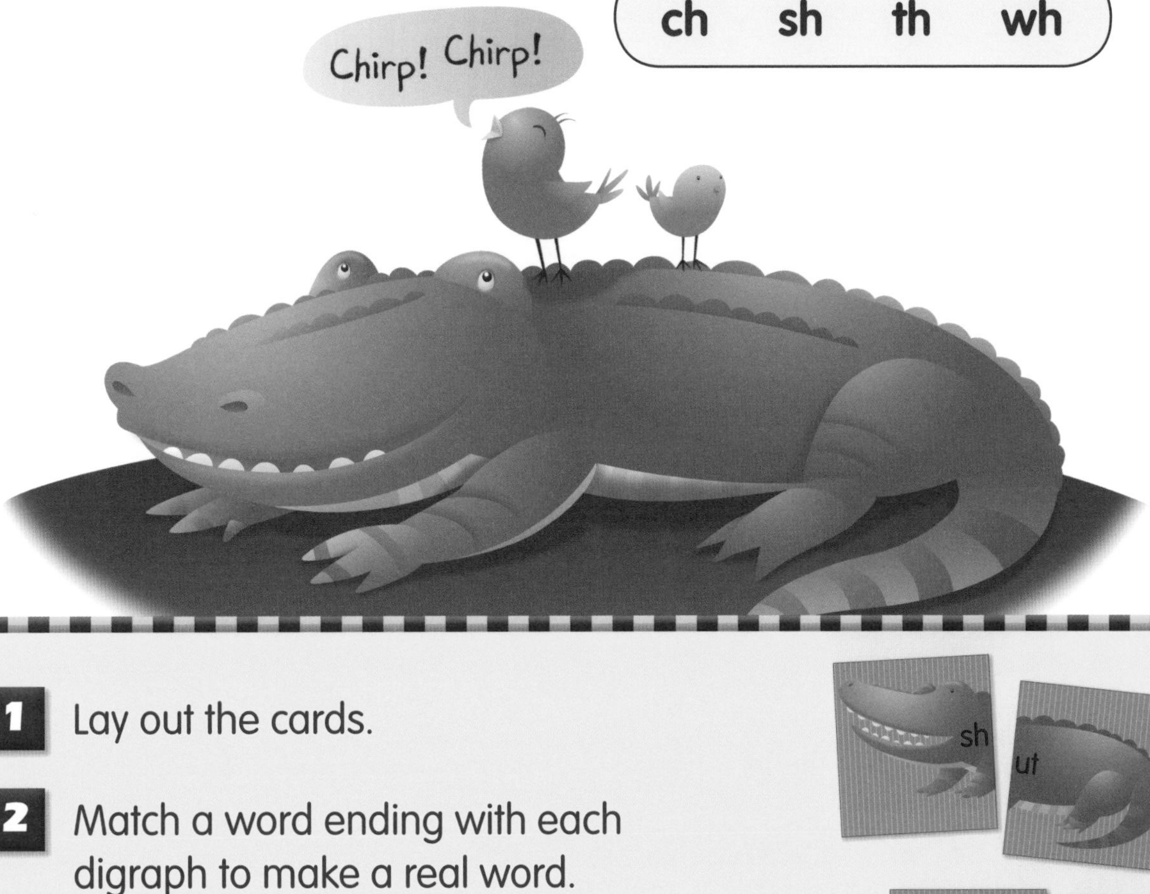

1. Lay out the cards.
2. Match a word ending with each digraph to make a real word.
3. Complete the response form.

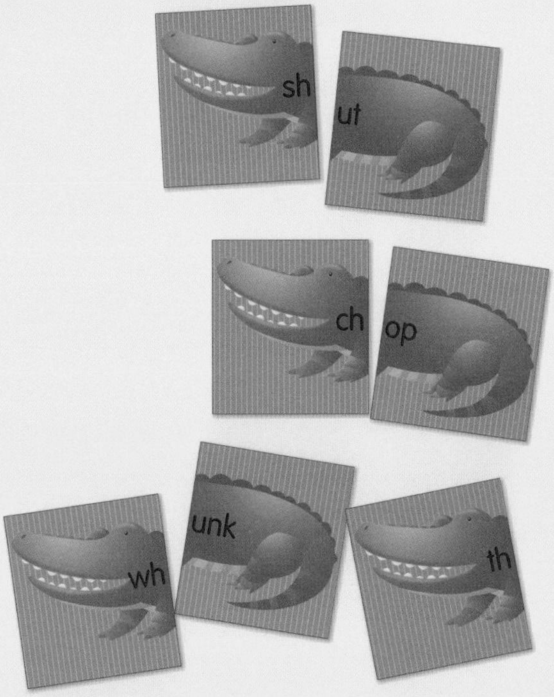

Make Words with Digraphs

Look at the cards. Add a word ending to complete the words.

Answers may vary.

ch
- ch op
- ch arm
- ch ip or eap
- ch ain or unk

sh
- sh oe
- sh oot
- sh ut or ape
- sh ell or eep

th
- th ink
- th ank
- th umb or ing
- th ick or ird

wh
- wh isk
- wh ale
- wh ite or eel
- wh eat or ere

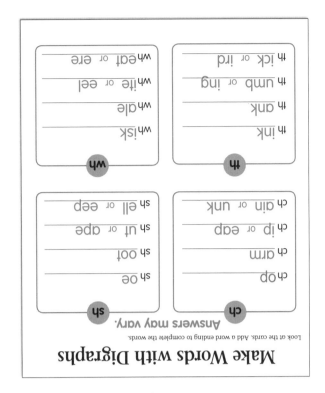

Response Form

(fold)

Answer Key

Make Words with Digraphs

Answers may vary.

Answer Key

Make Words with Digraphs

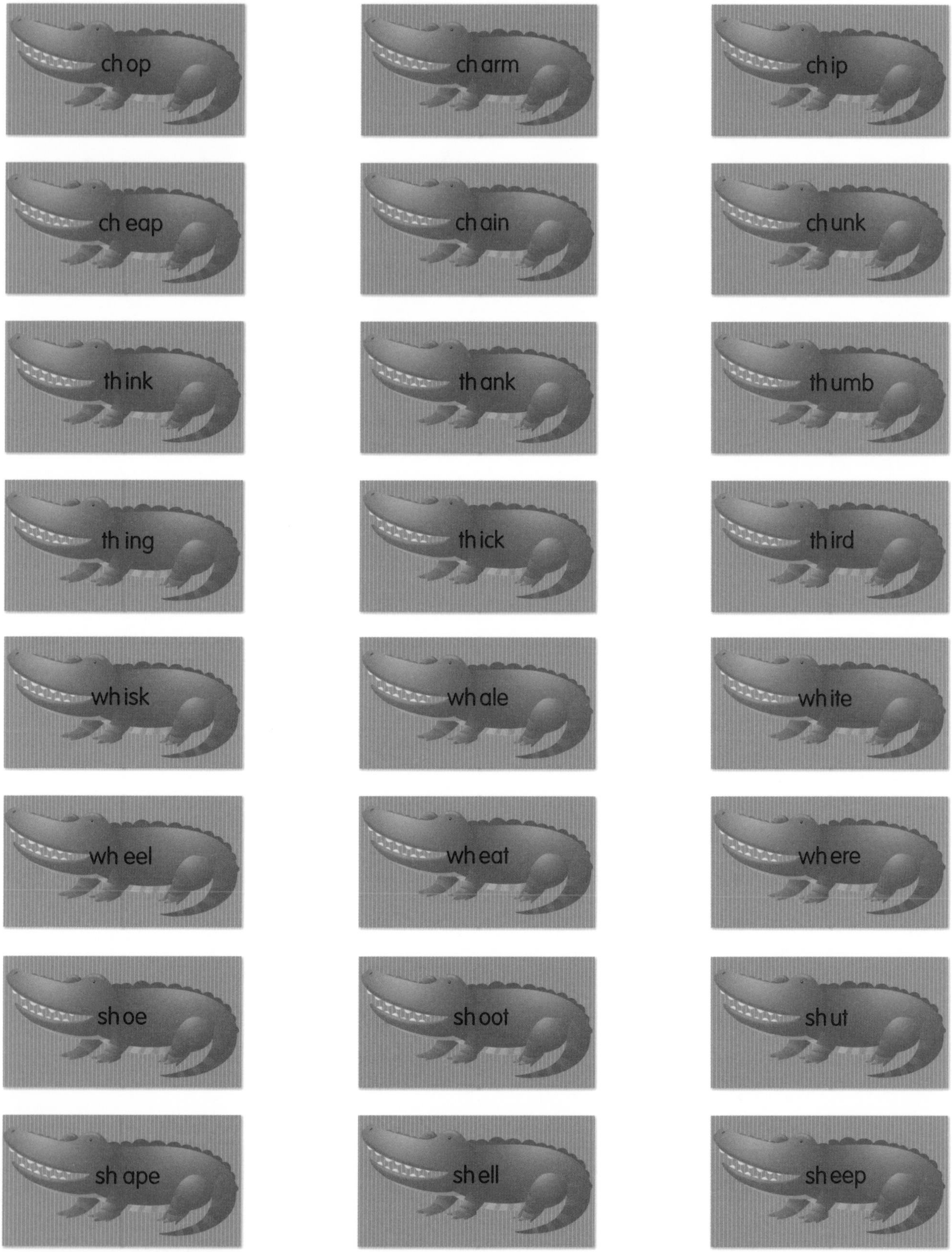

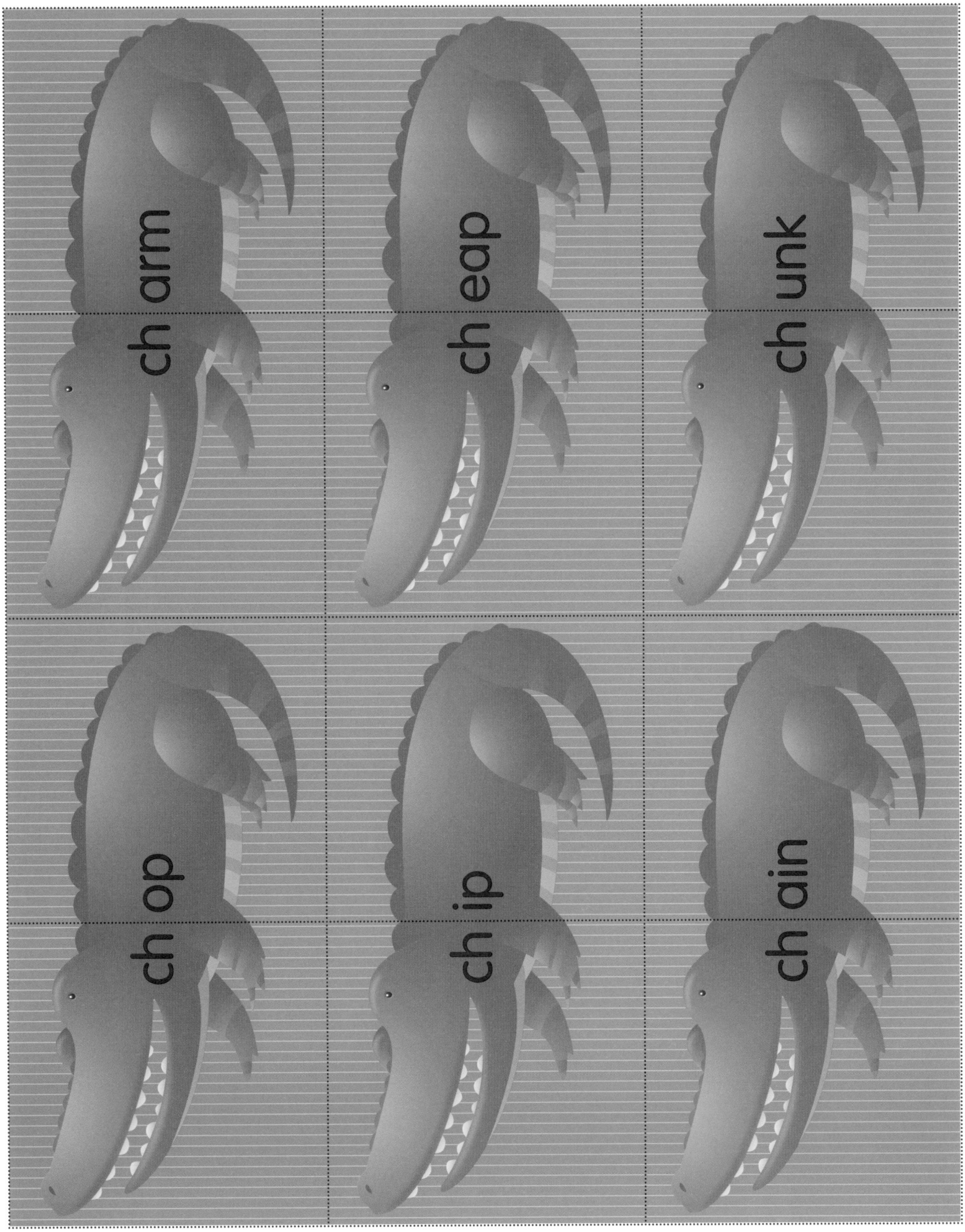
ch arm
ch eap
ch unk
ch op
ch ip
ch ain

Make Words with Digraphs

Take It to Your Seat Centers
Reading & Language
EMC 2842 • © Evan-Moor Corp.

Make Words with Digraphs

Take It to Your Seat Centers
Reading & Language
EMC 2842 • © Evan-Moor Corp.

Make Words with Digraphs

Take It to Your Seat Centers
Reading & Language
EMC 2842 • © Evan-Moor Corp.

Make Words with Digraphs

Take It to Your Seat Centers
Reading & Language
EMC 2842 • © Evan-Moor Corp.

Make Words with Digraphs

Take It to Your Seat Centers
Reading & Language
EMC 2842 • © Evan-Moor Corp.

Make Words with Digraphs

Take It to Your Seat Centers
Reading & Language
EMC 2842 • © Evan-Moor Corp.

Make Words with Digraphs

Take It to Your Seat Centers
Reading & Language
EMC 2842 • © Evan-Moor Corp.

Make Words with Digraphs

Take It to Your Seat Centers
Reading & Language
EMC 2842 • © Evan-Moor Corp.

Make Words with Digraphs

Take It to Your Seat Centers
Reading & Language
EMC 2842 • © Evan-Moor Corp.

Make Words with Digraphs

Take It to Your Seat Centers
Reading & Language
EMC 2842 • © Evan-Moor Corp.

Make Words with Digraphs

Take It to Your Seat Centers
Reading & Language
EMC 2842 • © Evan-Moor Corp.

Make Words with Digraphs

Take It to Your Seat Centers
Reading & Language
EMC 2842 • © Evan-Moor Corp.

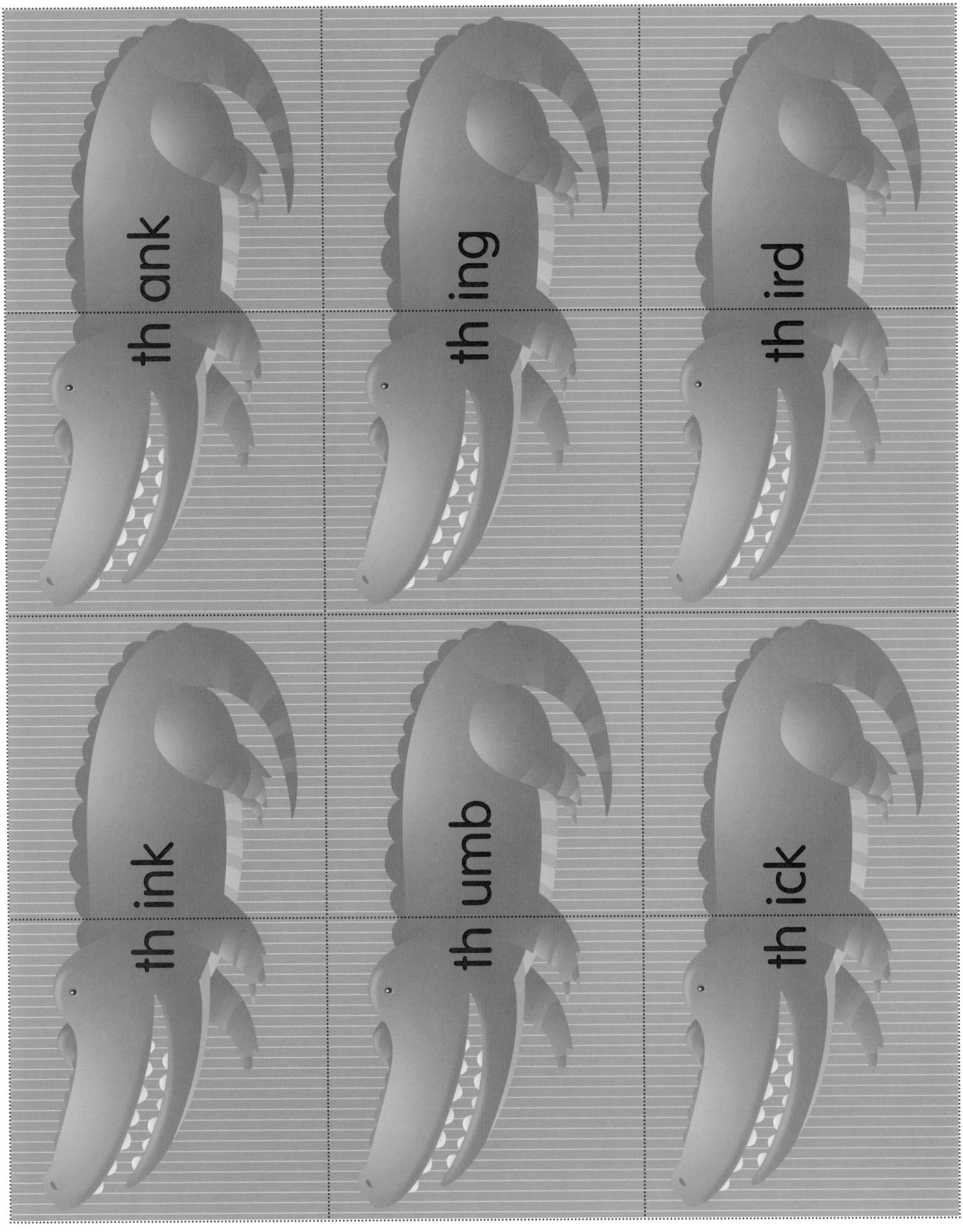
th ank
th ing
th ird
th ink
th umb
th ick

Make Words with Digraphs

Take It to Your Seat Centers
Reading & Language
EMC 2842 • © Evan-Moor Corp.

Make Words with Digraphs

Take It to Your Seat Centers
Reading & Language
EMC 2842 • © Evan-Moor Corp.

Make Words with Digraphs

Take It to Your Seat Centers
Reading & Language
EMC 2842 • © Evan-Moor Corp.

Make Words with Digraphs

Take It to Your Seat Centers
Reading & Language
EMC 2842 • © Evan-Moor Corp.

Make Words with Digraphs

Take It to Your Seat Centers
Reading & Language
EMC 2842 • © Evan-Moor Corp.

Make Words with Digraphs

Take It to Your Seat Centers
Reading & Language
EMC 2842 • © Evan-Moor Corp.

Make Words with Digraphs

Take It to Your Seat Centers
Reading & Language
EMC 2842 • © Evan-Moor Corp.

Make Words with Digraphs

Take It to Your Seat Centers
Reading & Language
EMC 2842 • © Evan-Moor Corp.

Make Words with Digraphs

Take It to Your Seat Centers
Reading & Language
EMC 2842 • © Evan-Moor Corp.

Make Words with Digraphs

Take It to Your Seat Centers
Reading & Language
EMC 2842 • © Evan-Moor Corp.

Make Words with Digraphs

Take It to Your Seat Centers
Reading & Language
EMC 2842 • © Evan-Moor Corp.

Make Words with Digraphs

Take It to Your Seat Centers
Reading & Language
EMC 2842 • © Evan-Moor Corp.

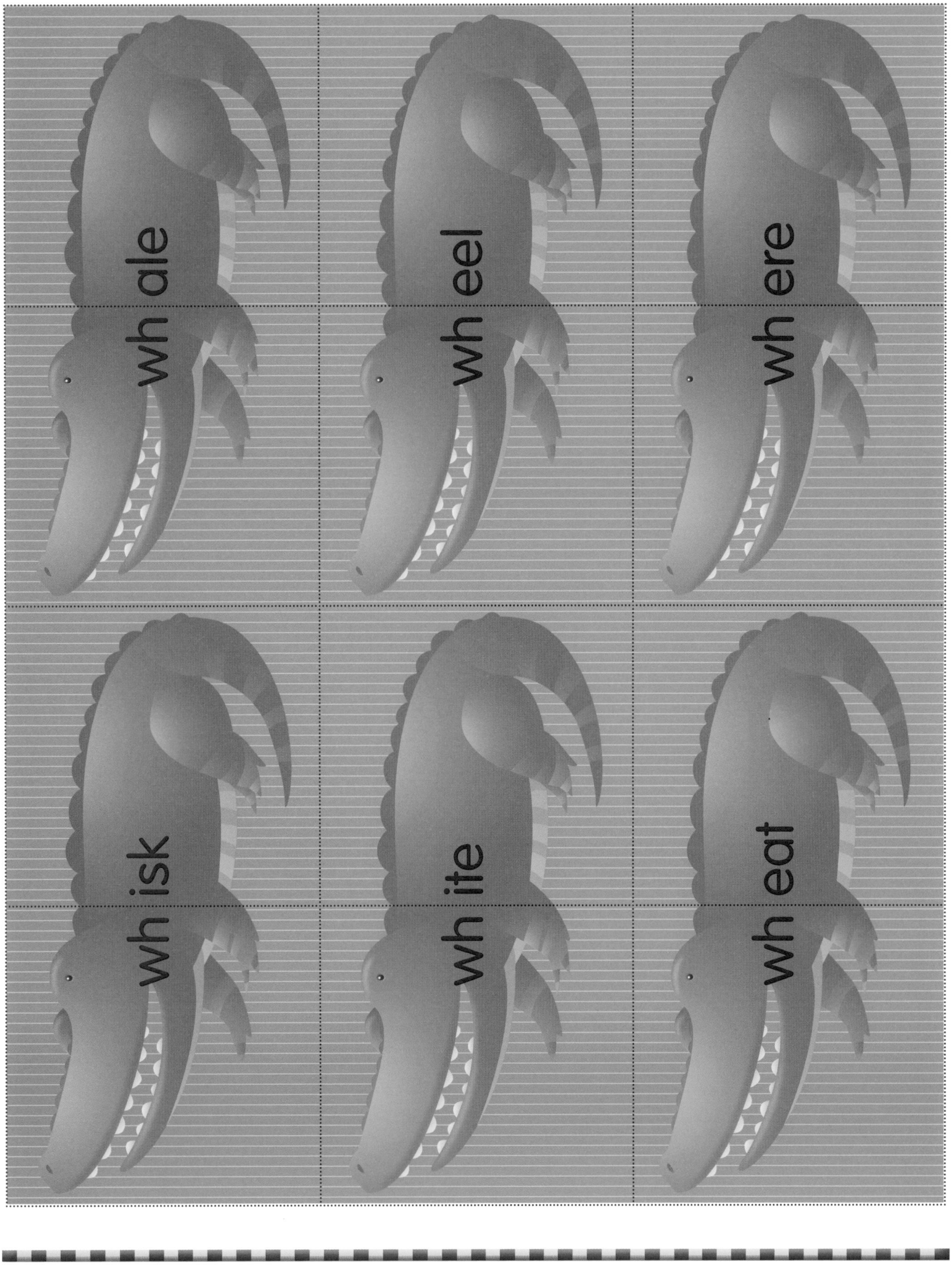
wh ale
wh eel
wh ere
wh isk
wh ite
wh eat

Make Words with Digraphs

Take It to Your Seat Centers
Reading & Language
EMC 2842 • © Evan-Moor Corp.

Make Words with Digraphs

Take It to Your Seat Centers
Reading & Language
EMC 2842 • © Evan-Moor Corp.

Make Words with Digraphs

Take It to Your Seat Centers
Reading & Language
EMC 2842 • © Evan-Moor Corp.

Make Words with Digraphs

Take It to Your Seat Centers
Reading & Language
EMC 2842 • © Evan-Moor Corp.

Make Words with Digraphs

Take It to Your Seat Centers
Reading & Language
EMC 2842 • © Evan-Moor Corp.

Make Words with Digraphs

Take It to Your Seat Centers
Reading & Language
EMC 2842 • © Evan-Moor Corp.

Make Words with Digraphs

Take It to Your Seat Centers
Reading & Language
EMC 2842 • © Evan-Moor Corp.

Make Words with Digraphs

Take It to Your Seat Centers
Reading & Language
EMC 2842 • © Evan-Moor Corp.

Make Words with Digraphs

Take It to Your Seat Centers
Reading & Language
EMC 2842 • © Evan-Moor Corp.

Make Words with Digraphs

Take It to Your Seat Centers
Reading & Language
EMC 2842 • © Evan-Moor Corp.

Make Words with Digraphs

Take It to Your Seat Centers
Reading & Language
EMC 2842 • © Evan-Moor Corp.

Make Words with Digraphs

Take It to Your Seat Centers
Reading & Language
EMC 2842 • © Evan-Moor Corp.

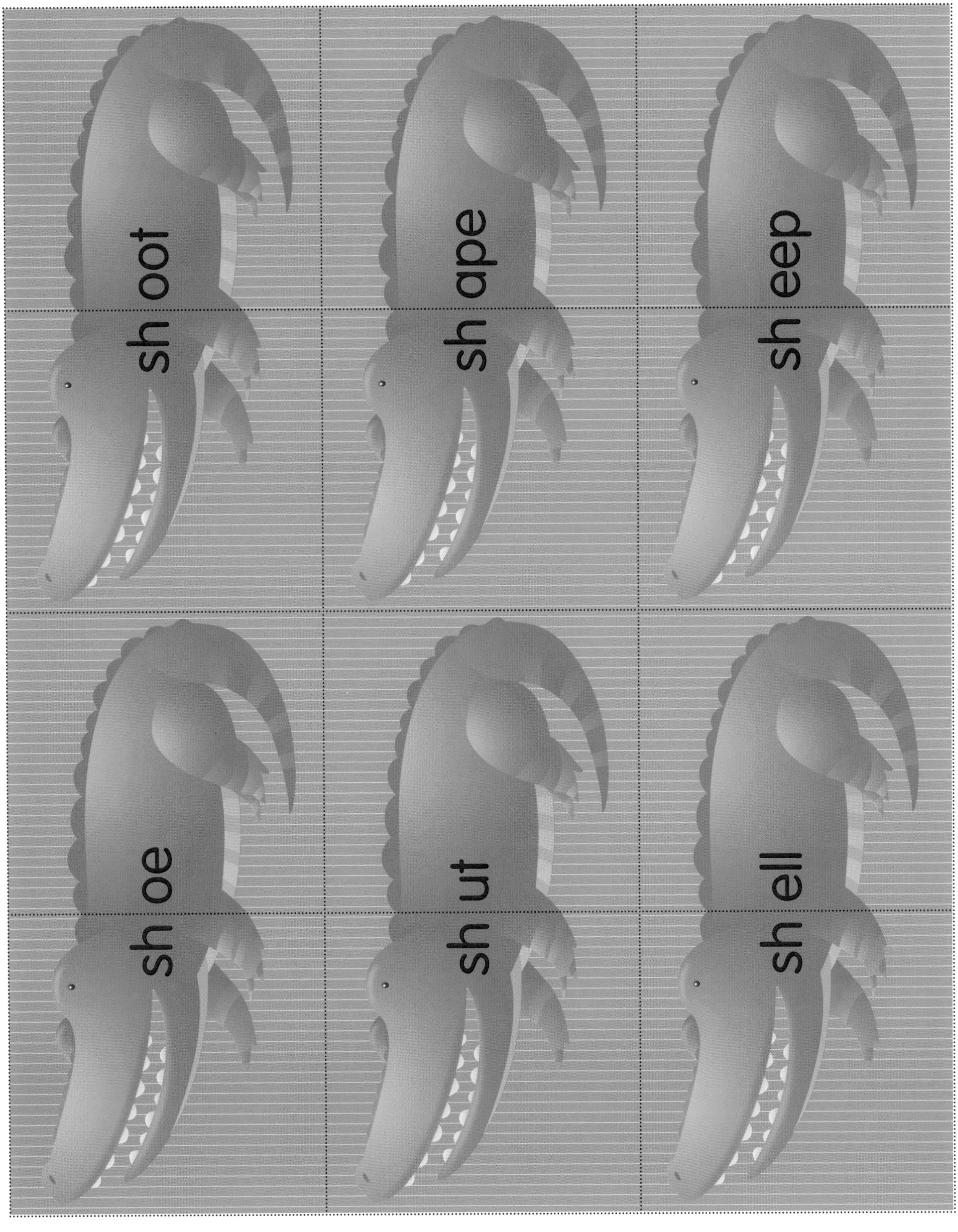
sh oot
sh ape
sh eep
sh oe
sh ut
sh ell

Make Words with Digraphs

Take It to Your Seat Centers
Reading & Language
EMC 2842 • © Evan-Moor Corp.

Make Words with Digraphs

Take It to Your Seat Centers
Reading & Language
EMC 2842 • © Evan-Moor Corp.

Make Words with Digraphs

Take It to Your Seat Centers
Reading & Language
EMC 2842 • © Evan-Moor Corp.

Make Words with Digraphs

Take It to Your Seat Centers
Reading & Language
EMC 2842 • © Evan-Moor Corp.

Make Words with Digraphs

Take It to Your Seat Centers
Reading & Language
EMC 2842 • © Evan-Moor Corp.

Make Words with Digraphs

Take It to Your Seat Centers
Reading & Language
EMC 2842 • © Evan-Moor Corp.

Make Words with Digraphs

Take It to Your Seat Centers
Reading & Language
EMC 2842 • © Evan-Moor Corp.

Make Words with Digraphs

Take It to Your Seat Centers
Reading & Language
EMC 2842 • © Evan-Moor Corp.

Make Words with Digraphs

Take It to Your Seat Centers
Reading & Language
EMC 2842 • © Evan-Moor Corp.

Make Words with Digraphs

Take It to Your Seat Centers
Reading & Language
EMC 2842 • © Evan-Moor Corp.

Make Words with Digraphs

Take It to Your Seat Centers
Reading & Language
EMC 2842 • © Evan-Moor Corp.

Make Words with Digraphs

Take It to Your Seat Centers
Reading & Language
EMC 2842 • © Evan-Moor Corp.

Take It to Your Seat Centers

Listen for Long Vowels

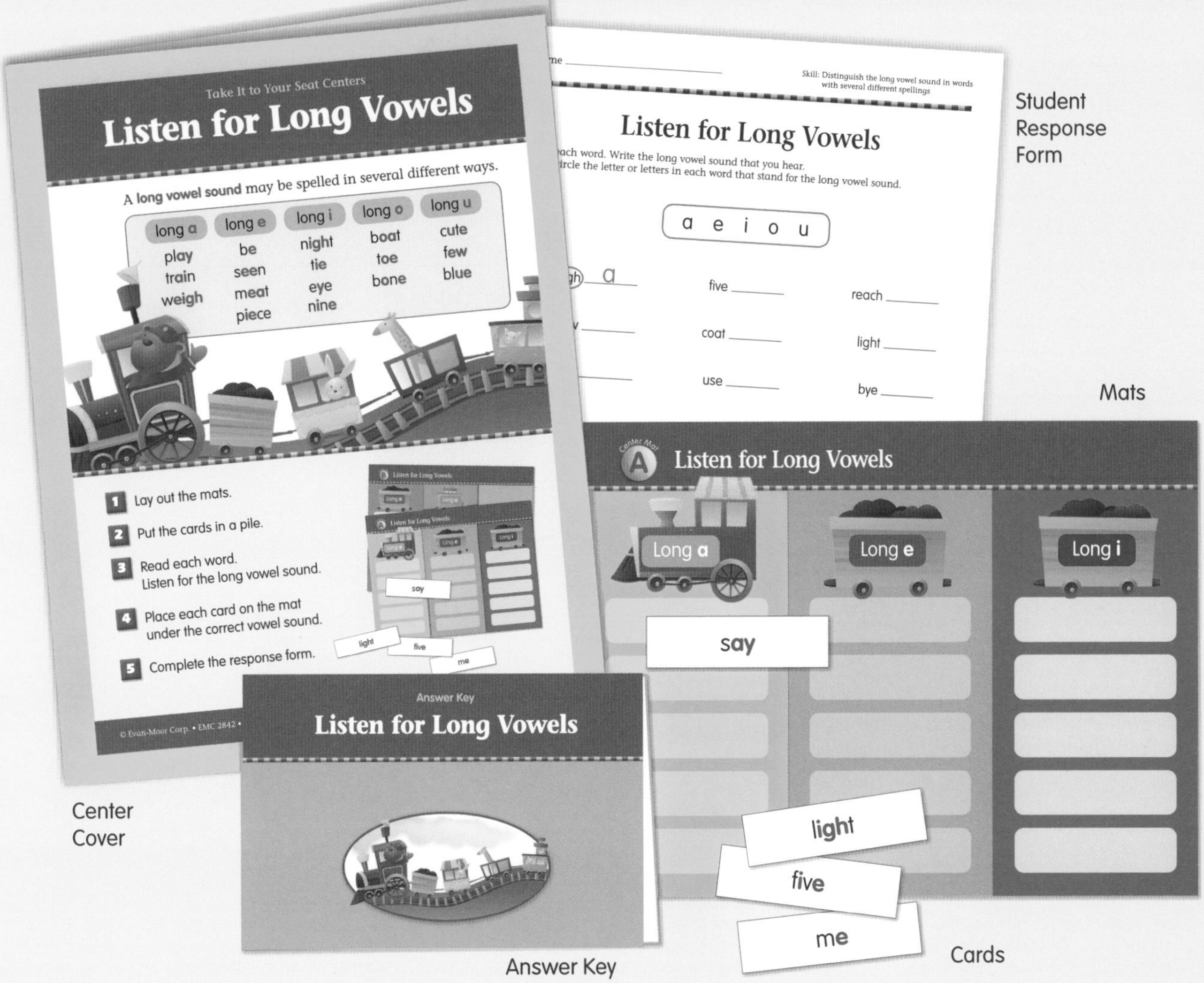

Student Response Form

Mats

Center Cover

Answer Key

Cards

Skill
Distinguish the long vowel sound in words with several different spellings

Prepare the Center
Follow the directions on page 3.

Introduce the Center
Demonstrate how to use the center. State the goal: *You will listen for the long vowel sound in each word and place the card on the mat under the correct vowel.*

Name ______________________

Skill: Distinguish the long vowel sound in words with several different spellings

Listen for Long Vowels

Read each word. Write the long vowel sound that you hear.
Then circle the letter or letters in each word that stand for the long vowel sound.

a e i o u

sleigh a	five ______	reach ______
slow ______	coat ______	light ______
break ______	use ______	bye ______
tail ______	cry ______	toast ______
toe ______	cute ______	they ______
chief ______	pie ______	joke ______
happy ______	true ______	tray ______
deep ______	unit ______	show ______

Listen for Long Vowels

A **long vowel sound** may be spelled in several different ways.

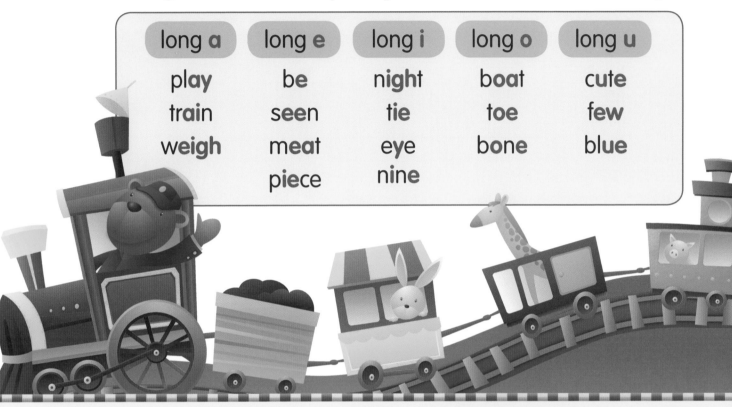

long a	long e	long i	long o	long u
play	be	night	boat	cute
train	seen	tie	toe	few
weigh	meat	eye	bone	blue
	piece	nine		

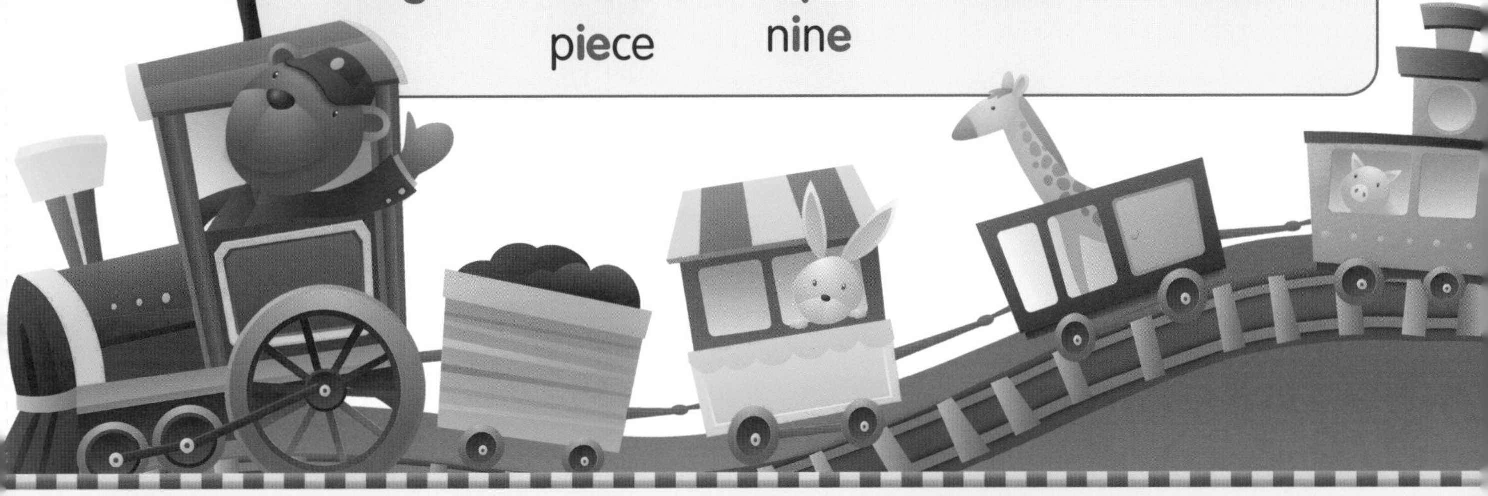

1. Lay out the mats.
2. Put the cards in a pile.
3. Read each word.
   Listen for the long vowel sound.
4. Place each card on the mat
   under the correct vowel sound.
5. Complete the response form.

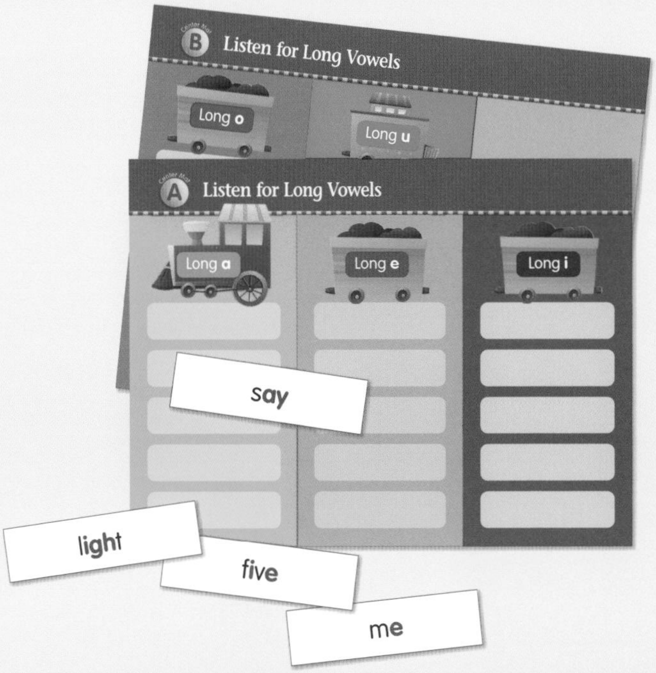

Answer Key

Listen for Long Vowels

(fold)

Response Form

Listen for Long Vowels

Read each word. Write the long vowel sound that you hear.
Then circle the letter or letters in each word that stand for the long vowel sound.

a e i o u

sleigh a	five i	reach e
slow o	coat o	light i
break a	use u	bye i
tail a	cry i	toast o
toe o	cute u	they a
chief e	pie i	joke o
happy e	true u	tray a
deep e	unit u	show o

Answer Key

Listen for Long Vowels

A

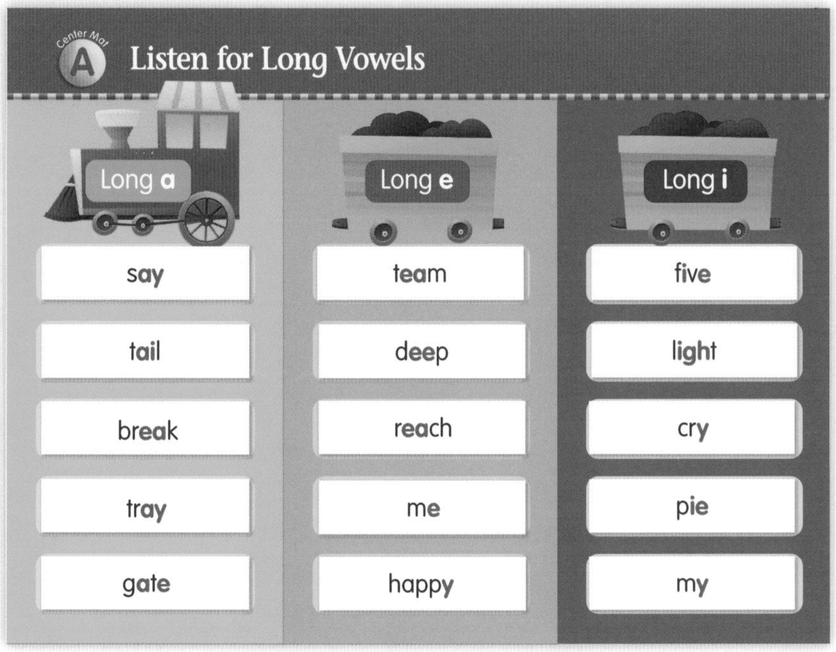

B

Center Mat A

Listen for Long Vowels

Center Mat B

Listen for Long Vowels

say	tray	break
tail	gate	me
happy	deep	reach
team	cry	pie
five	light	my
go	toe	joke
coat	slow	cute
use	grew	unit
cube		

Listen for Long Vowels
Take It to Your Seat Centers
Reading & Language
EMC 2842 • © Evan-Moor Corp.

Listen for Long Vowels
Take It to Your Seat Centers
Reading & Language
EMC 2842 • © Evan-Moor Corp.

Listen for Long Vowels
Take It to Your Seat Centers
Reading & Language
EMC 2842 • © Evan-Moor Corp.

Listen for Long Vowels
Take It to Your Seat Centers
Reading & Language
EMC 2842 • © Evan-Moor Corp.

Listen for Long Vowels
Take It to Your Seat Centers
Reading & Language
EMC 2842 • © Evan-Moor Corp.

Listen for Long Vowels
Take It to Your Seat Centers
Reading & Language
EMC 2842 • © Evan-Moor Corp.

Listen for Long Vowels
Take It to Your Seat Centers
Reading & Language
EMC 2842 • © Evan-Moor Corp.

Listen for Long Vowels
Take It to Your Seat Centers
Reading & Language
EMC 2842 • © Evan-Moor Corp.

Listen for Long Vowels
Take It to Your Seat Centers
Reading & Language
EMC 2842 • © Evan-Moor Corp.

Listen for Long Vowels
Take It to Your Seat Centers
Reading & Language
EMC 2842 • © Evan-Moor Corp.

Listen for Long Vowels
Take It to Your Seat Centers
Reading & Language
EMC 2842 • © Evan-Moor Corp.

Listen for Long Vowels
Take It to Your Seat Centers
Reading & Language
EMC 2842 • © Evan-Moor Corp.

Listen for Long Vowels
Take It to Your Seat Centers
Reading & Language
EMC 2842 • © Evan-Moor Corp.

Listen for Long Vowels
Take It to Your Seat Centers
Reading & Language
EMC 2842 • © Evan-Moor Corp.

Listen for Long Vowels
Take It to Your Seat Centers
Reading & Language
EMC 2842 • © Evan-Moor Corp.

Listen for Long Vowels
Take It to Your Seat Centers
Reading & Language
EMC 2842 • © Evan-Moor Corp.

Listen for Long Vowels
Take It to Your Seat Centers
Reading & Language
EMC 2842 • © Evan-Moor Corp.

Listen for Long Vowels
Take It to Your Seat Centers
Reading & Language
EMC 2842 • © Evan-Moor Corp.

Listen for Long Vowels
Take It to Your Seat Centers
Reading & Language
EMC 2842 • © Evan-Moor Corp.

Listen for Long Vowels
Take It to Your Seat Centers
Reading & Language
EMC 2842 • © Evan-Moor Corp.

Listen for Long Vowels
Take It to Your Seat Centers
Reading & Language
EMC 2842 • © Evan-Moor Corp.

Listen for Long Vowels
Take It to Your Seat Centers
Reading & Language
EMC 2842 • © Evan-Moor Corp.

Listen for Long Vowels
Take It to Your Seat Centers
Reading & Language
EMC 2842 • © Evan-Moor Corp.

Listen for Long Vowels
Take It to Your Seat Centers
Reading & Language
EMC 2842 • © Evan-Moor Corp.

Listen for Long Vowels
Take It to Your Seat Centers
Reading & Language
EMC 2842 • © Evan-Moor Corp.

Take It to Your Seat Centers

Alphabetical Order

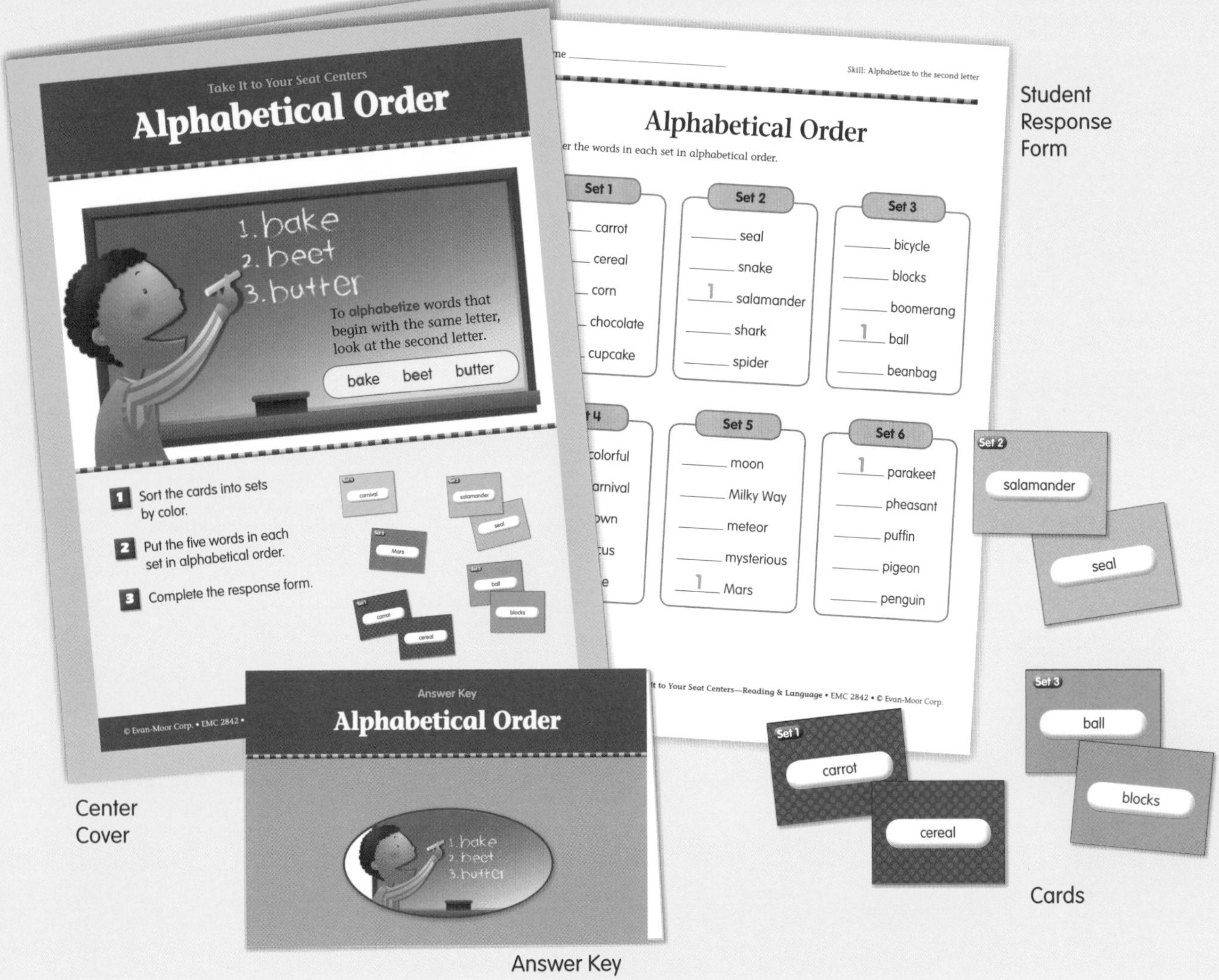

Skill
Alphabetize to the second letter

Prepare the Center
Follow the directions on page 3.

Introduce the Center
Demonstrate how to use the center. State the goal: *You will sort the cards by color and then put each set of cards in alphabetical order.*

Name ____________________ Skill: Alphabetize to the second letter

Alphabetical Order

Number the words in each set in alphabetical order.

Set 1

1 carrot
___ cereal
___ corn
___ chocolate
___ cupcake

Set 2

___ seal
___ snake
1 salamander
___ shark
___ spider

Set 3

___ bicycle
___ blocks
___ boomerang
1 ball
___ beanbag

Set 4

___ colorful
1 carnival
___ clown
___ circus
___ cycle

Set 5

___ moon
___ Milky Way
___ meteor
___ mysterious
1 Mars

Set 6

1 parakeet
___ pheasant
___ puffin
___ pigeon
___ penguin

Alphabetical Order

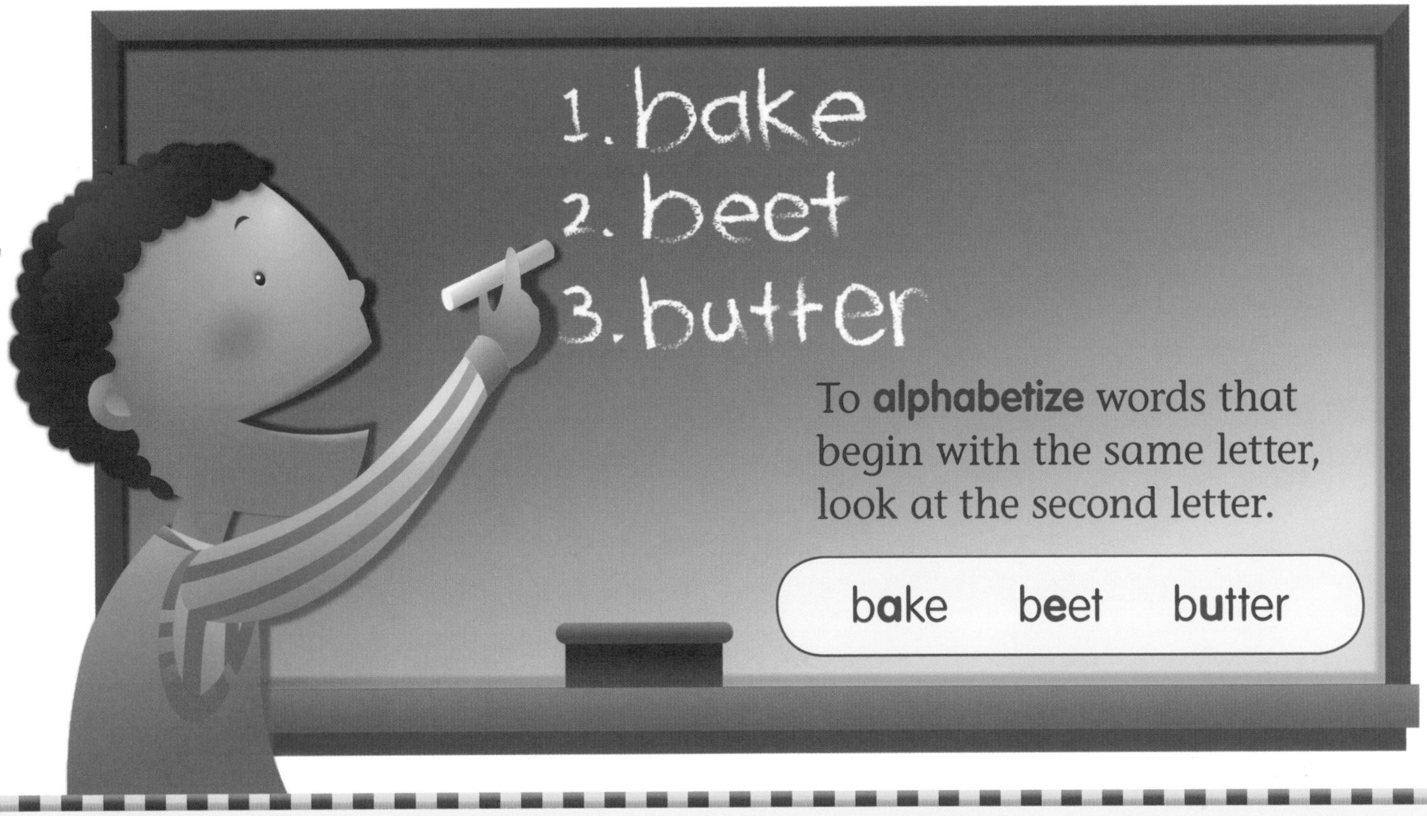

1. bake
2. beet
3. butter
To **alphabetize** words that begin with the same letter, look at the second letter.
bake beet butter

1. Sort the cards into sets by color.
2. Put the five words in each set in alphabetical order.
3. Complete the response form.

Response Form

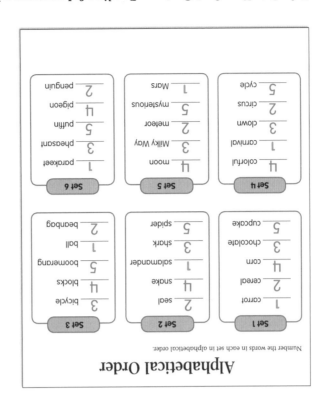

Alphabetical Order

Number the words in each set in alphabetical order.

Set 1
1 carrot
2 cereal
4 corn
3 chocolate
5 cupcake

Set 2
2 seal
4 snake
1 salamander
3 shark
5 spider

Set 3
3 bicycle
4 blocks
5 boomerang
1 ball
2 beanbag

Set 4
4 colorful
1 carnival
3 clown
2 circus
5 cycle

Set 5
4 moon
3 Milky Way
2 meteor
5 mysterious
1 Mars

Set 6
1 parakeet
3 pheasant
5 puffin
4 pigeon
2 penguin

(fold)

Answer Key

Alphabetical Order

Answer Key

Alphabetical Order

Set 1
- carrot
- cereal
- chocolate
- corn
- cupcake

Set 2
- salamander
- seal
- shark
- snake
- spider

Set 3
- ball
- beanbag
- bicycle
- blocks
- boomerang

Set 4
- carnival
- circus
- clown
- colorful
- cycle

Set 5
- Mars
- meteor
- Milky Way
- moon
- mysterious

Set 6
- parakeet
- penguin
- pheasant
- pigeon
- puffin

Set 1	Set 2	Set 3
carrot	salamander	ball
cupcake	seal	blocks
cereal	spider	bicycle
chocolate	shark	boomerang
corn	snake	beanbag

Alphabetical Order

Take It to Your Seat Centers
Reading & Language
EMC 2842 • © Evan-Moor Corp.

Alphabetical Order

Take It to Your Seat Centers
Reading & Language
EMC 2842 • © Evan-Moor Corp.

Alphabetical Order

Take It to Your Seat Centers
Reading & Language
EMC 2842 • © Evan-Moor Corp.

Alphabetical Order

Take It to Your Seat Centers
Reading & Language
EMC 2842 • © Evan-Moor Corp.

Alphabetical Order

Take It to Your Seat Centers
Reading & Language
EMC 2842 • © Evan-Moor Corp.

Alphabetical Order

Take It to Your Seat Centers
Reading & Language
EMC 2842 • © Evan-Moor Corp.

Alphabetical Order

Take It to Your Seat Centers
Reading & Language
EMC 2842 • © Evan-Moor Corp.

Alphabetical Order

Take It to Your Seat Centers
Reading & Language
EMC 2842 • © Evan-Moor Corp.

Alphabetical Order

Take It to Your Seat Centers
Reading & Language
EMC 2842 • © Evan-Moor Corp.

Alphabetical Order

Take It to Your Seat Centers
Reading & Language
EMC 2842 • © Evan-Moor Corp.

Alphabetical Order

Take It to Your Seat Centers
Reading & Language
EMC 2842 • © Evan-Moor Corp.

Alphabetical Order

Take It to Your Seat Centers
Reading & Language
EMC 2842 • © Evan-Moor Corp.

Alphabetical Order

Take It to Your Seat Centers
Reading & Language
EMC 2842 • © Evan-Moor Corp.

Alphabetical Order

Take It to Your Seat Centers
Reading & Language
EMC 2842 • © Evan-Moor Corp.

Alphabetical Order

Take It to Your Seat Centers
Reading & Language
EMC 2842 • © Evan-Moor Corp.

Set 4	Set 5	Set 6
carnival	Mars	parakeet
clown	moon	penguin
circus	meteor	puffin
colorful	Milky Way	pheasant
cycle	mysterious	pigeon

Alphabetical Order

Take It to Your Seat Centers
Reading & Language
EMC 2842 • © Evan-Moor Corp.

Alphabetical Order

Take It to Your Seat Centers
Reading & Language
EMC 2842 • © Evan-Moor Corp.

Alphabetical Order

Take It to Your Seat Centers
Reading & Language
EMC 2842 • © Evan-Moor Corp.

Alphabetical Order

Take It to Your Seat Centers
Reading & Language
EMC 2842 • © Evan-Moor Corp.

Alphabetical Order

Take It to Your Seat Centers
Reading & Language
EMC 2842 • © Evan-Moor Corp.

Alphabetical Order

Take It to Your Seat Centers
Reading & Language
EMC 2842 • © Evan-Moor Corp.

Alphabetical Order

Take It to Your Seat Centers
Reading & Language
EMC 2842 • © Evan-Moor Corp.

Alphabetical Order

Take It to Your Seat Centers
Reading & Language
EMC 2842 • © Evan-Moor Corp.

Alphabetical Order

Take It to Your Seat Centers
Reading & Language
EMC 2842 • © Evan-Moor Corp.

Alphabetical Order

Take It to Your Seat Centers
Reading & Language
EMC 2842 • © Evan-Moor Corp.

Alphabetical Order

Take It to Your Seat Centers
Reading & Language
EMC 2842 • © Evan-Moor Corp.

Alphabetical Order

Take It to Your Seat Centers
Reading & Language
EMC 2842 • © Evan-Moor Corp.

Alphabetical Order

Take It to Your Seat Centers
Reading & Language
EMC 2842 • © Evan-Moor Corp.

Alphabetical Order

Take It to Your Seat Centers
Reading & Language
EMC 2842 • © Evan-Moor Corp.

Alphabetical Order

Take It to Your Seat Centers
Reading & Language
EMC 2842 • © Evan-Moor Corp.

Parts of a Sentence

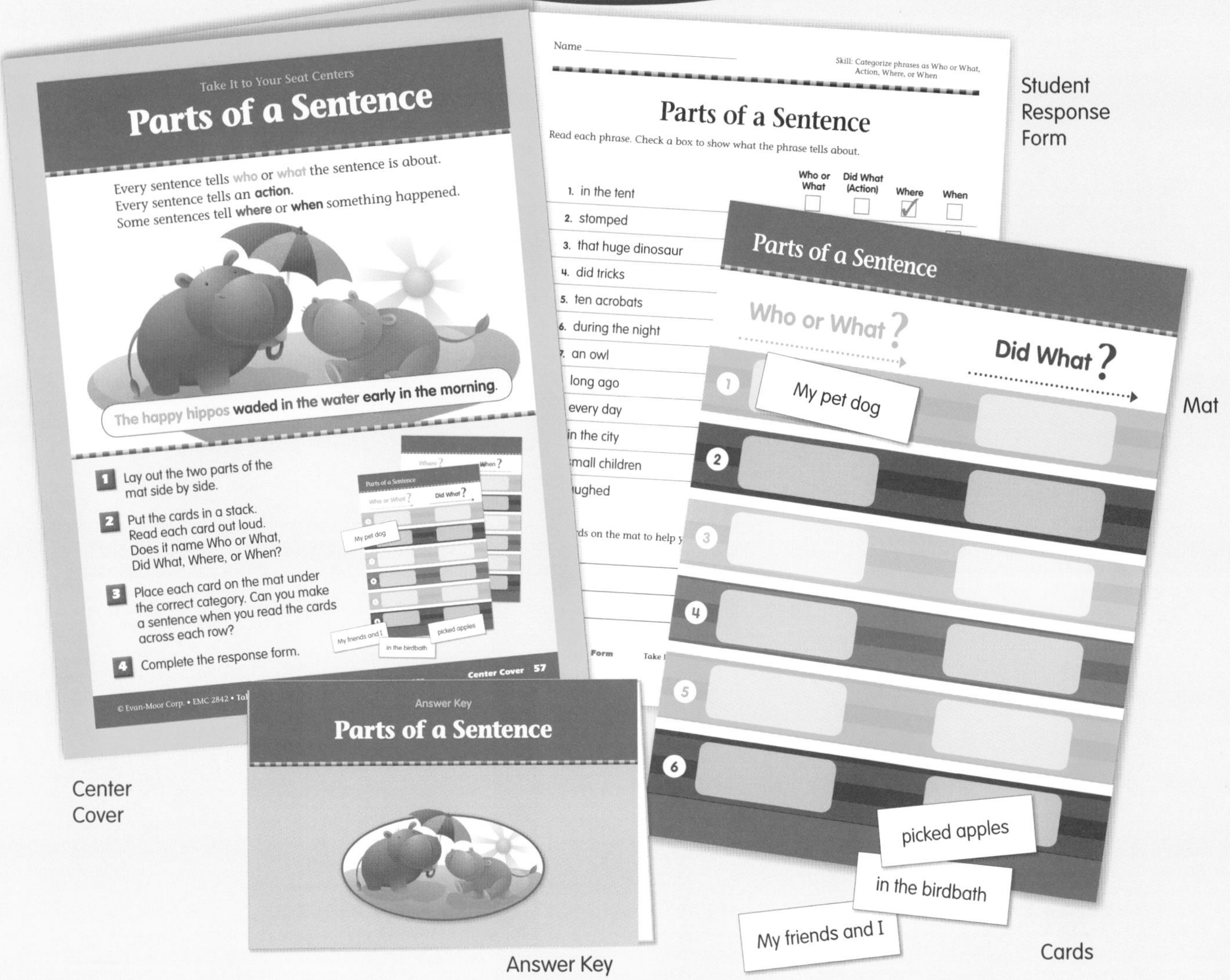

Skill
Categorize phrases as Who or What, Action, Where, or When

Prepare the Center
Follow the directions on page 3.

Introduce the Center
Demonstrate how to use the center. State the goal: *You will decide if each sentence part tells about who or what, the action, or where or when it happened.*

Name ____________________

Skill: Categorize phrases as Who or What, Action, Where, or When

Parts of a Sentence

Read each phrase. Check a box to show what the phrase tells about.

	Who or What	Did What (Action)	Where	When
1. in the tent	☐	☐	☑	☐
2. stomped	☐	☐	☐	☐
3. that huge dinosaur	☐	☐	☐	☐
4. did tricks	☐	☐	☐	☐
5. ten acrobats	☐	☐	☐	☐
6. during the night	☐	☐	☐	☐
7. an owl	☐	☐	☐	☐
8. long ago	☐	☐	☐	☐
9. every day	☐	☐	☐	☐
10. in the city	☐	☐	☐	☐
11. small children	☐	☐	☐	☐
12. laughed	☐	☐	☐	☐

Use the cards on the mat to help you write a complete sentence.

____

____

____

Parts of a Sentence

Every sentence tells who or what the sentence is about.
Every sentence tells an **action**.
Some sentences tell **where** or **when** something happened.

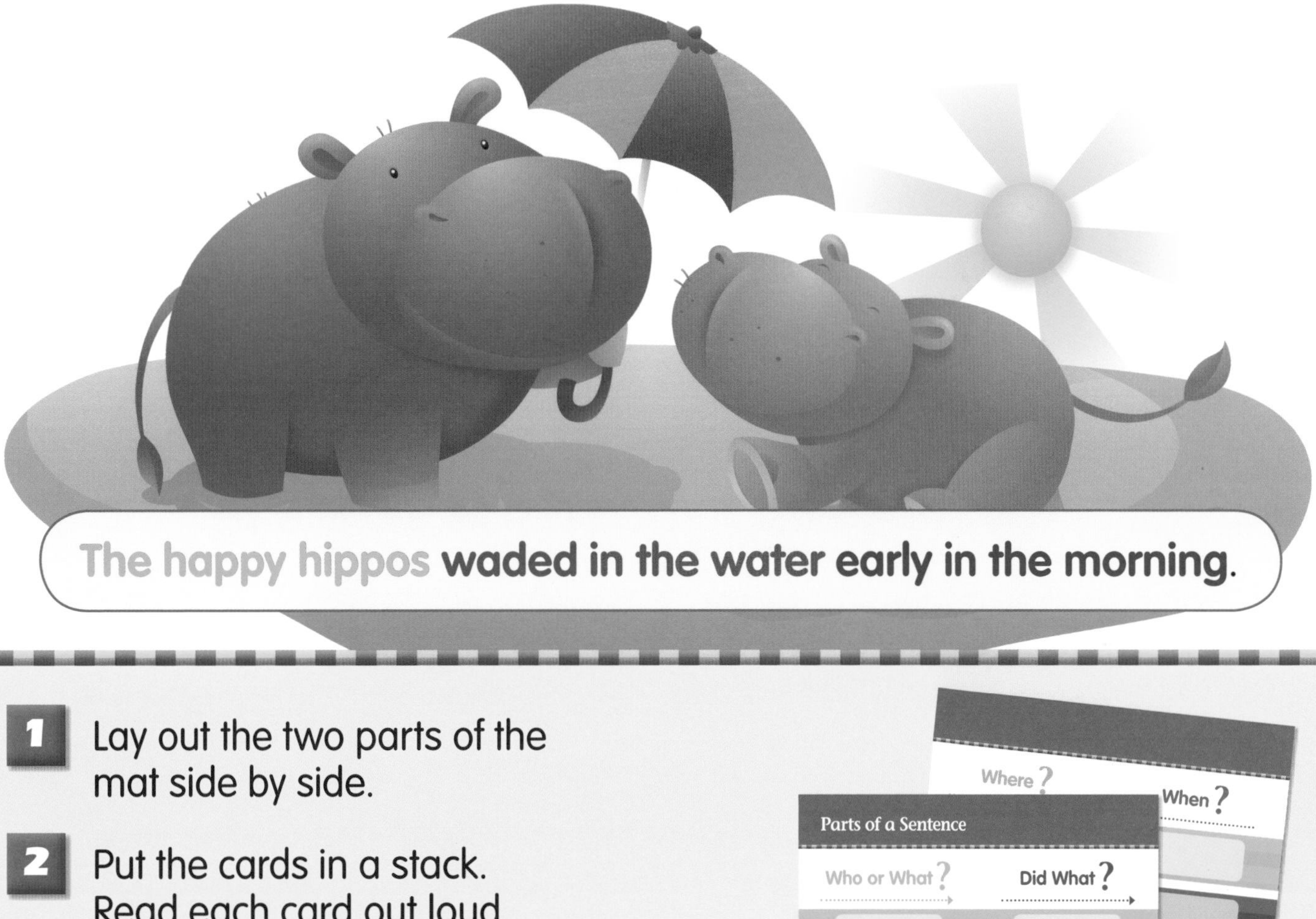
The happy hippos **waded in the water early in the morning**.

1. Lay out the two parts of the mat side by side.
2. Put the cards in a stack. Read each card out loud. Does it name Who or What, Did What, Where, or When?
3. Place each card on the mat under the correct category. Can you make a sentence when you read the cards across each row?
4. Complete the response form.

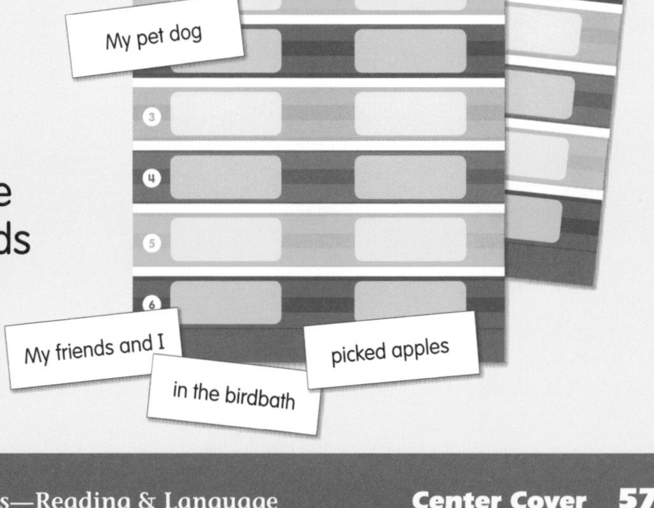

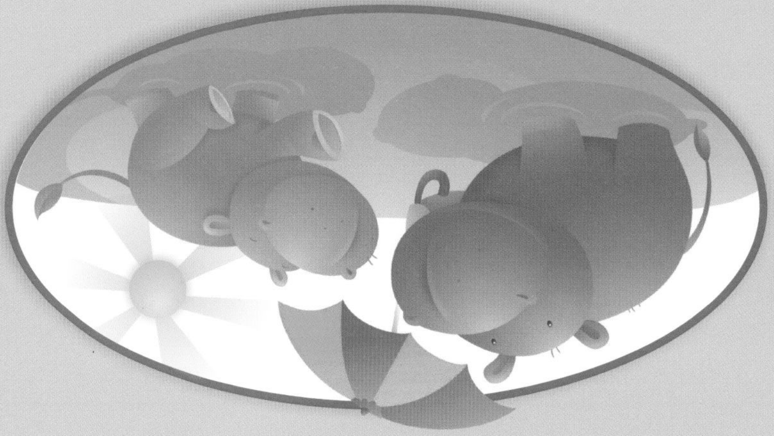

Parts of a Sentence

Answer Key

(fold)

Response Form

Parts of a Sentence

Read each phrase. Check a box to show what the phrase tells about.

	Who or What	Did What (Action)	Where	When
1. in the tent			✓	
2. stomped		✓		
3. that huge dinosaur	✓			
4. did tricks		✓		
5. ten acrobats	✓			
6. during the night				✓
7. an owl	✓			
8. long ago				✓
9. every day				✓
10. in the city			✓	
11. small children	✓			
12. laughed		✓		

Use the cards on the mat to help you write a complete sentence.

Answers will vary.

Answer Key

Parts of a Sentence

Parts of a Sentence

	Who or What?	Did What?	Where?	When?
1	My friends and I	picked apples	up in the treetops	after school
2	My pet dog	dug a hole	in the backyard	this morning
3	A green parrot	splashed	in the birdbath	every day
4	A huge dinosaur	stomped	through the jungle	long ago
5	That lazy giant	fell asleep	behind the castle	late one night
6	Ten acrobats	did tricks	in the tent	during the circus

Answers may vary.

Parts of a Sentence

	Who or What?	Did What?
1		
2		
3		
4		
5		
6		

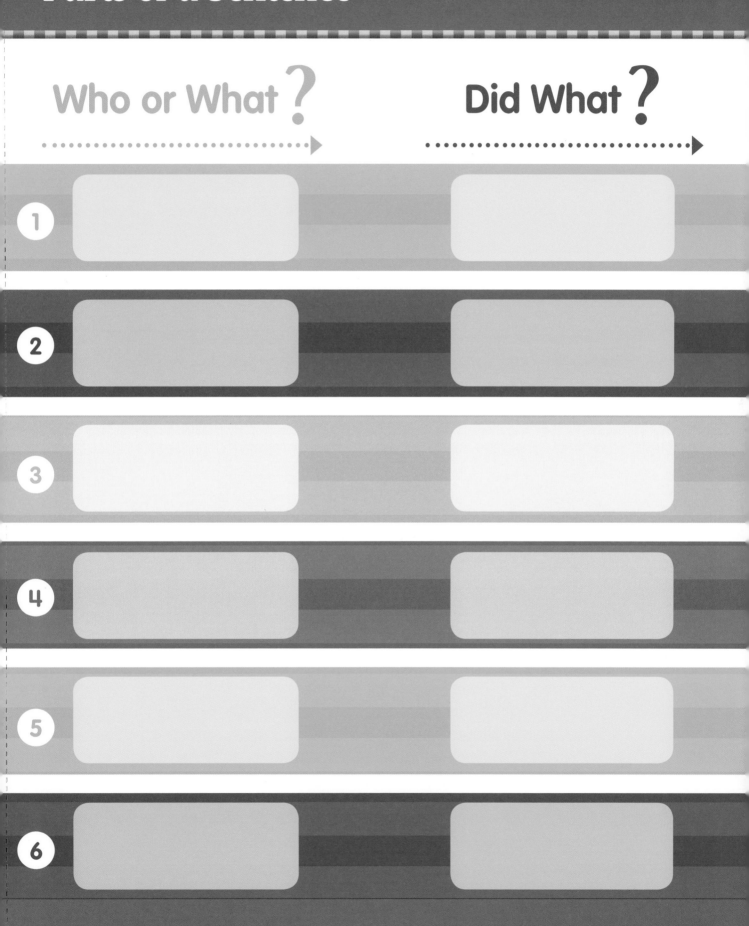

Where ?

When ?

My friends and I	picked apples	up in the treetops
after school	My pet dog	dug a hole
in the backyard	this morning	A green parrot
splashed	in the birdbath	every day
A huge dinosaur	stomped	through the jungle
long ago	That lazy giant	fell asleep
behind the castle	late one night	Ten acrobats
did tricks	in the tent	during the circus

Parts of a Sentence

Take It to Your Seat Centers
Reading & Language
EMC 2842 • © Evan-Moor Corp.

Parts of a Sentence

Take It to Your Seat Centers
Reading & Language
EMC 2842 • © Evan-Moor Corp.

Parts of a Sentence

Take It to Your Seat Centers
Reading & Language
EMC 2842 • © Evan-Moor Corp.

Parts of a Sentence

Take It to Your Seat Centers
Reading & Language
EMC 2842 • © Evan-Moor Corp.

Parts of a Sentence

Take It to Your Seat Centers
Reading & Language
EMC 2842 • © Evan-Moor Corp.

Parts of a Sentence

Take It to Your Seat Centers
Reading & Language
EMC 2842 • © Evan-Moor Corp.

Parts of a Sentence

Take It to Your Seat Centers
Reading & Language
EMC 2842 • © Evan-Moor Corp.

Parts of a Sentence

Take It to Your Seat Centers
Reading & Language
EMC 2842 • © Evan-Moor Corp.

Parts of a Sentence

Take It to Your Seat Centers
Reading & Language
EMC 2842 • © Evan-Moor Corp.

Parts of a Sentence

Take It to Your Seat Centers
Reading & Language
EMC 2842 • © Evan-Moor Corp.

Parts of a Sentence

Take It to Your Seat Centers
Reading & Language
EMC 2842 • © Evan-Moor Corp.

Parts of a Sentence

Take It to Your Seat Centers
Reading & Language
EMC 2842 • © Evan-Moor Corp.

Parts of a Sentence

Take It to Your Seat Centers
Reading & Language
EMC 2842 • © Evan-Moor Corp.

Parts of a Sentence

Take It to Your Seat Centers
Reading & Language
EMC 2842 • © Evan-Moor Corp.

Parts of a Sentence

Take It to Your Seat Centers
Reading & Language
EMC 2842 • © Evan-Moor Corp.

Parts of a Sentence

Take It to Your Seat Centers
Reading & Language
EMC 2842 • © Evan-Moor Corp.

Parts of a Sentence

Take It to Your Seat Centers
Reading & Language
EMC 2842 • © Evan-Moor Corp.

Parts of a Sentence

Take It to Your Seat Centers
Reading & Language
EMC 2842 • © Evan-Moor Corp.

Parts of a Sentence

Take It to Your Seat Centers
Reading & Language
EMC 2842 • © Evan-Moor Corp.

Parts of a Sentence

Take It to Your Seat Centers
Reading & Language
EMC 2842 • © Evan-Moor Corp.

Parts of a Sentence

Take It to Your Seat Centers
Reading & Language
EMC 2842 • © Evan-Moor Corp.

Parts of a Sentence

Take It to Your Seat Centers
Reading & Language
EMC 2842 • © Evan-Moor Corp.

Parts of a Sentence

Take It to Your Seat Centers
Reading & Language
EMC 2842 • © Evan-Moor Corp.

Take It to Your Seat Centers

More Than One

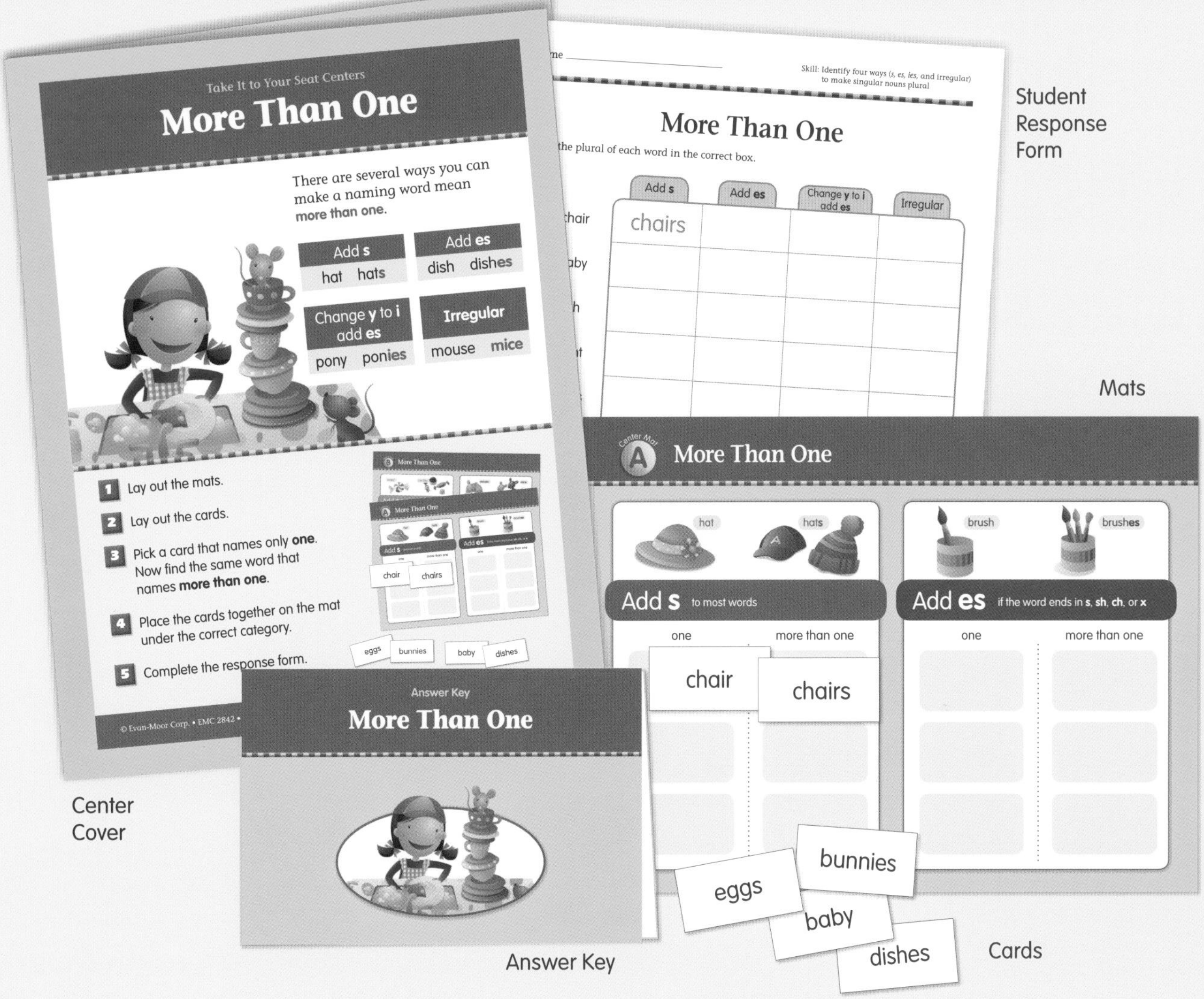

Skill
Identify four ways (*s, es, ies,* and irregular) to make singular nouns plural

Prepare the Center
Follow the directions on page 3.

Introduce the Center
Demonstrate how to use the center. State the goal: *You will match pairs of words that name "one" and "more than one" and then place them on the mat under the correct rule.*

Name ______________________

Skill: Identify four ways (*s, es, ies,* and irregular) to make singular nouns plural

More Than One

Write the plural of each word in the correct box.

	Add **s**	Add **es**	Change **y** to **i** add **es**	Irregular
1. chair	chairs			
2. baby				
3. dish				
4. plant				
5. dress				
6. clock				
7. cherry				
8. woman				
9. box				
10. foot				

Take It to Your Seat Centers

More Than One

There are several ways you can make a naming word mean **more than one**.

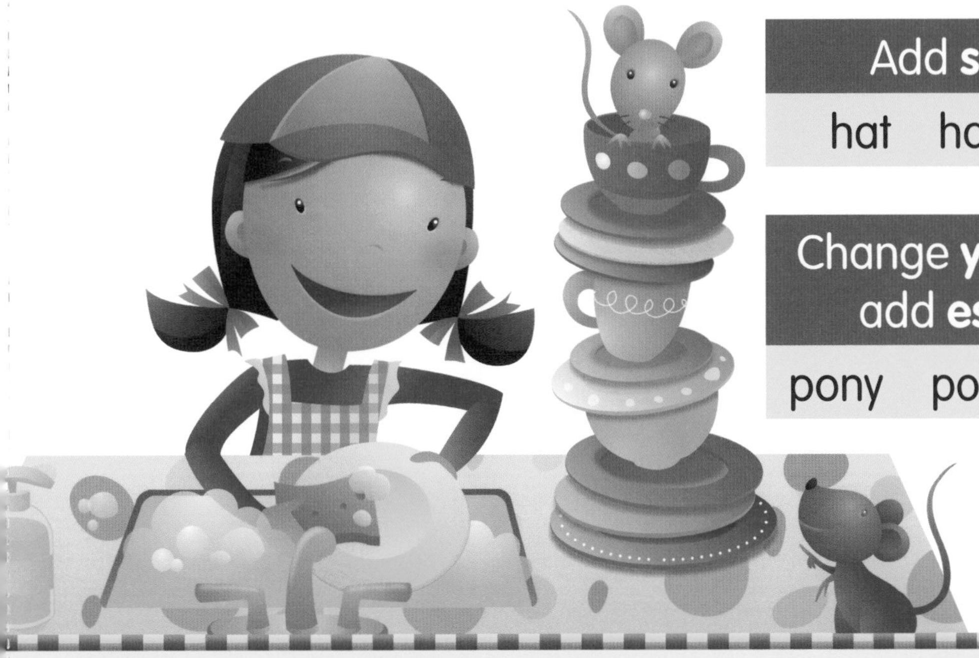

Add **s**	Add **es**
hat hats	dish dishes

Change **y** to **i** add **es**	**Irregular**
pony ponies	mouse **mice**

1. Lay out the mats.
2. Lay out the cards.
3. Pick a card that names only **one**. Now find the same word that names **more than one**.
4. Place the cards together on the mat under the correct category.
5. Complete the response form.

More Than One

Answer Key

(fold)

Response Form

More Than One

Write the plural of each word in the correct box.

	Add s	Add es	Change y to i add es	Irregular
1. chair	chairs			
2. baby			babies	
3. dish		dishes		
4. plant	plants			
5. dress		dresses		
6. clock	clocks			
7. cherry			cherries	
8. woman				women
9. box		boxes		
10. foot				feet

Answer Key

More Than One

A

Center Mat A — More Than One

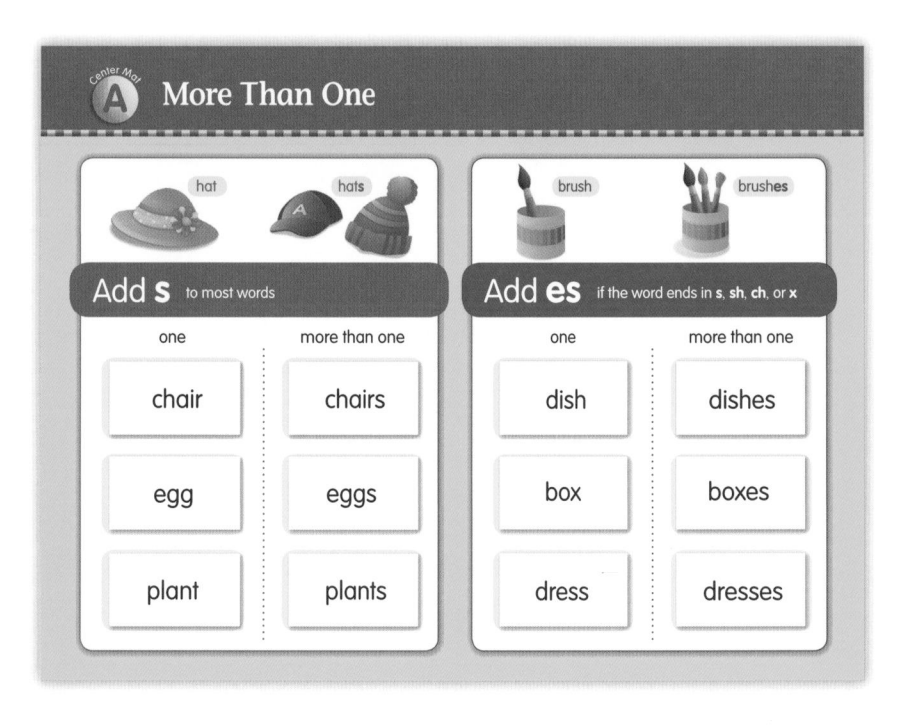

Add s to most words

one	more than one
chair	chairs
egg	eggs
plant	plants

Add es if the word ends in **s**, **sh**, **ch**, or **x**

one	more than one
dish	dishes
box	boxes
dress	dresses

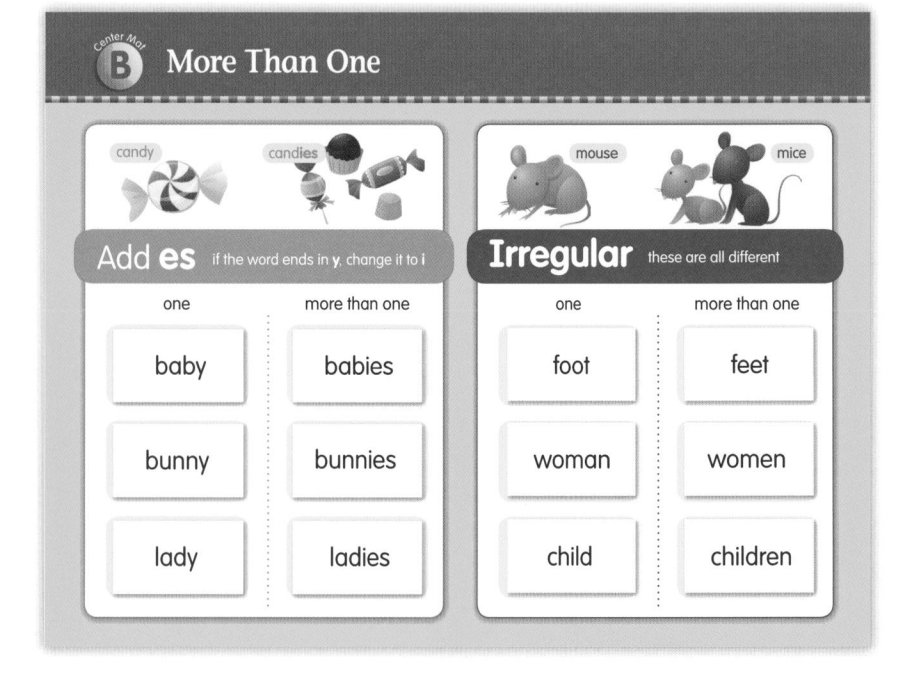

B

Center Mat B — More Than One

Add es if the word ends in **y**, change it to **i**

one	more than one
baby	babies
bunny	bunnies
lady	ladies

Irregular these are all different

one	more than one
foot	feet
woman	women
child	children

Center Mat A

More Than One

Add **s** to most words

one	more than one

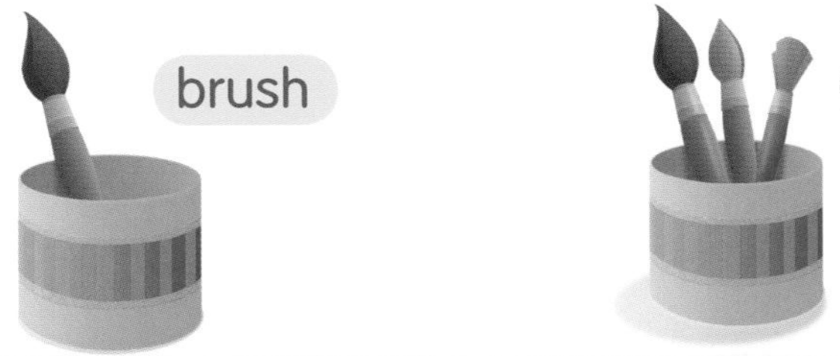

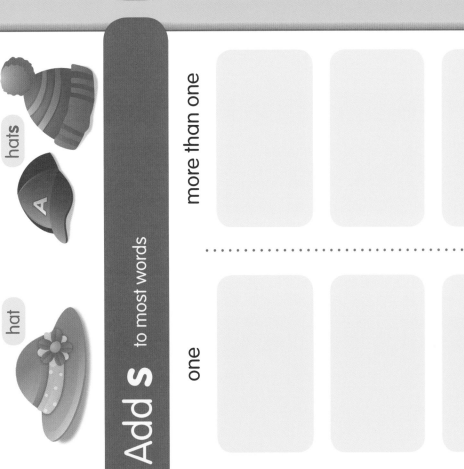

Add **es** if the word ends in **s**, **sh**, **ch**, or **x**

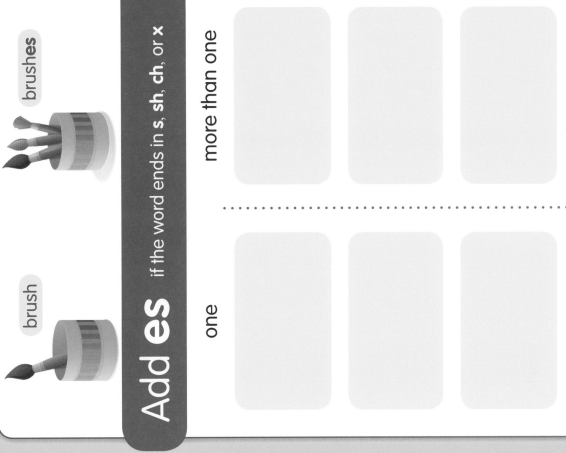

one	more than one

Center Mat B

More Than One

Add **es** if the word ends in **y**, change it to **i**

one	more than one

Irregular these are all different

one	more than one

chair	chairs	egg
eggs	plant	plants
baby	babies	bunny
bunnies	lady	ladies
dish	dishes	box
boxes	dress	dresses
foot	feet	woman
women	child	children

More Than One Take It to Your Seat Centers Reading & Language EMC 2842 • © Evan-Moor Corp.	**More Than One** Take It to Your Seat Centers Reading & Language EMC 2842 • © Evan-Moor Corp.	**More Than One** Take It to Your Seat Centers Reading & Language EMC 2842 • © Evan-Moor Corp.
More Than One Take It to Your Seat Centers Reading & Language EMC 2842 • © Evan-Moor Corp.	**More Than One** Take It to Your Seat Centers Reading & Language EMC 2842 • © Evan-Moor Corp.	**More Than One** Take It to Your Seat Centers Reading & Language EMC 2842 • © Evan-Moor Corp.
More Than One Take It to Your Seat Centers Reading & Language EMC 2842 • © Evan-Moor Corp.	**More Than One** Take It to Your Seat Centers Reading & Language EMC 2842 • © Evan-Moor Corp.	**More Than One** Take It to Your Seat Centers Reading & Language EMC 2842 • © Evan-Moor Corp.
More Than One Take It to Your Seat Centers Reading & Language EMC 2842 • © Evan-Moor Corp.	**More Than One** Take It to Your Seat Centers Reading & Language EMC 2842 • © Evan-Moor Corp.	**More Than One** Take It to Your Seat Centers Reading & Language EMC 2842 • © Evan-Moor Corp.
More Than One Take It to Your Seat Centers Reading & Language EMC 2842 • © Evan-Moor Corp.	**More Than One** Take It to Your Seat Centers Reading & Language EMC 2842 • © Evan-Moor Corp.	**More Than One** Take It to Your Seat Centers Reading & Language EMC 2842 • © Evan-Moor Corp.
More Than One Take It to Your Seat Centers Reading & Language EMC 2842 • © Evan-Moor Corp.	**More Than One** Take It to Your Seat Centers Reading & Language EMC 2842 • © Evan-Moor Corp.	**More Than One** Take It to Your Seat Centers Reading & Language EMC 2842 • © Evan-Moor Corp.
More Than One Take It to Your Seat Centers Reading & Language EMC 2842 • © Evan-Moor Corp.	**More Than One** Take It to Your Seat Centers Reading & Language EMC 2842 • © Evan-Moor Corp.	**More Than One** Take It to Your Seat Centers Reading & Language EMC 2842 • © Evan-Moor Corp.
More Than One Take It to Your Seat Centers Reading & Language EMC 2842 • © Evan-Moor Corp.	**More Than One** Take It to Your Seat Centers Reading & Language EMC 2842 • © Evan-Moor Corp.	**More Than One** Take It to Your Seat Centers Reading & Language EMC 2842 • © Evan-Moor Corp.

Synonyms

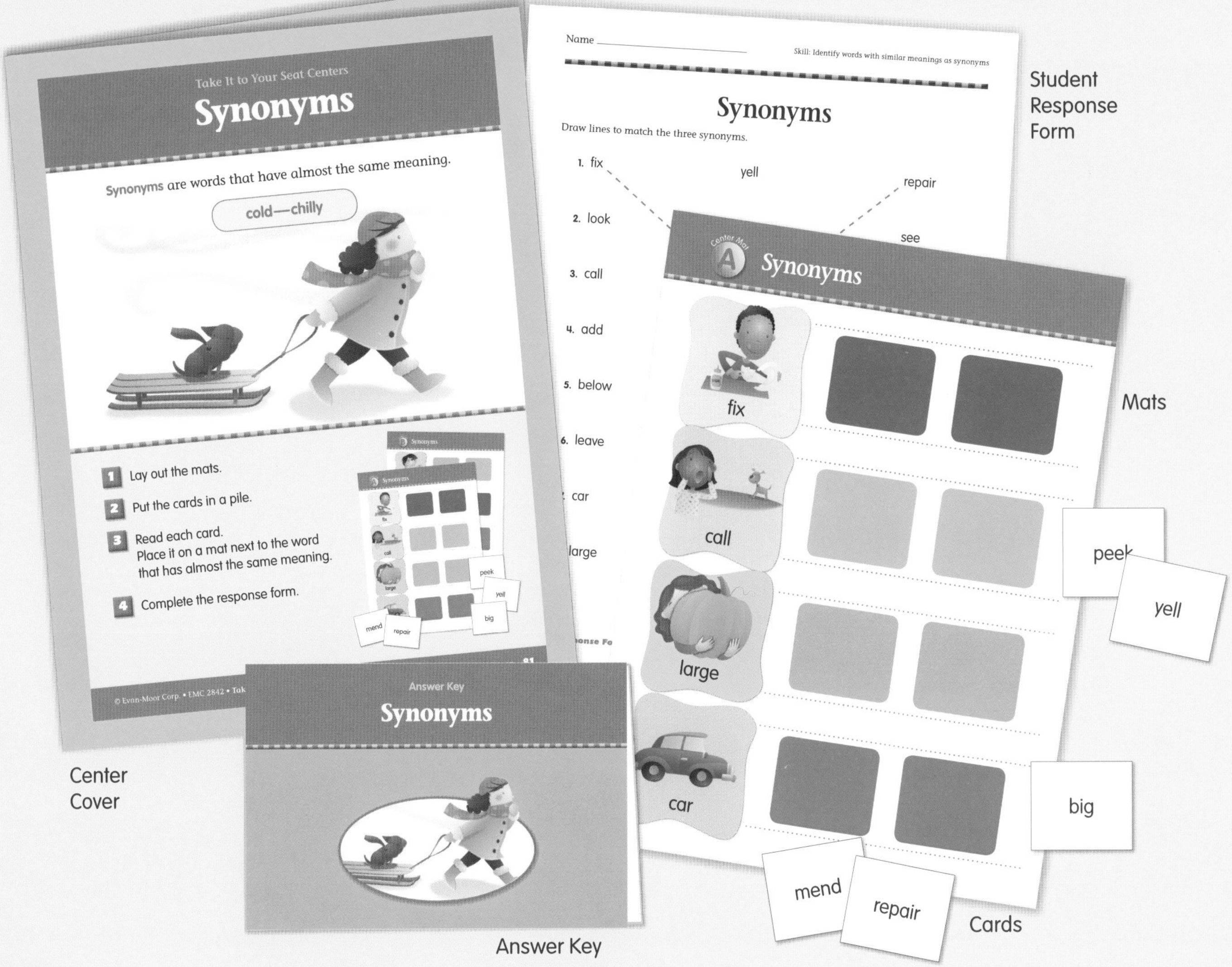

Skill
Identify words with similar meanings as synonyms

Prepare the Center
Follow the directions on page 3.

Introduce the Center
Demonstrate how to use the center. State the goal: *You will find two word cards that mean about the same as the words on the mats.*

Name ______________________ Skill: Identify words with similar meanings as synonyms

Synonyms

Draw lines to match the three synonyms.

1. fix	yell	repair
2. look	sum up	see
3. call	mend	shout
4. add	auto	vehicle
5. below	peek	total
6. leave	under	exit
7. car	huge	big
8. large	go	beneath

Synonyms

Synonyms are words that have almost the same meaning.

cold—chilly

1. Lay out the mats.
2. Put the cards in a pile.
3. Read each card.
   Place it on a mat next to the word
   that has almost the same meaning.
4. Complete the response form.

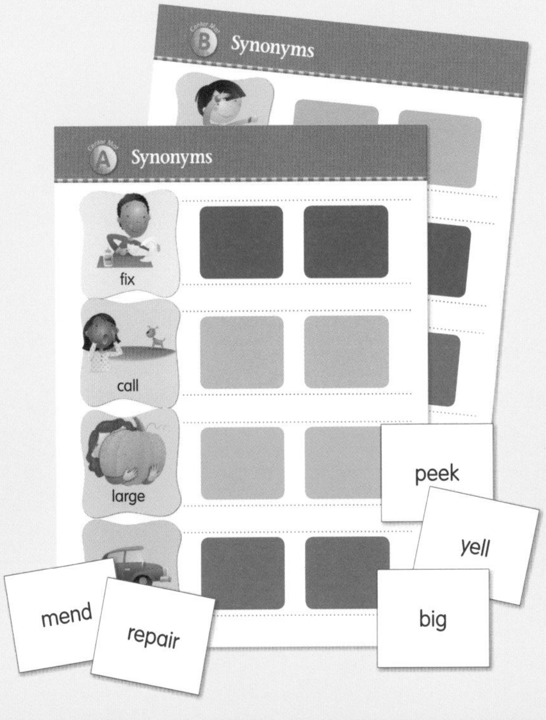

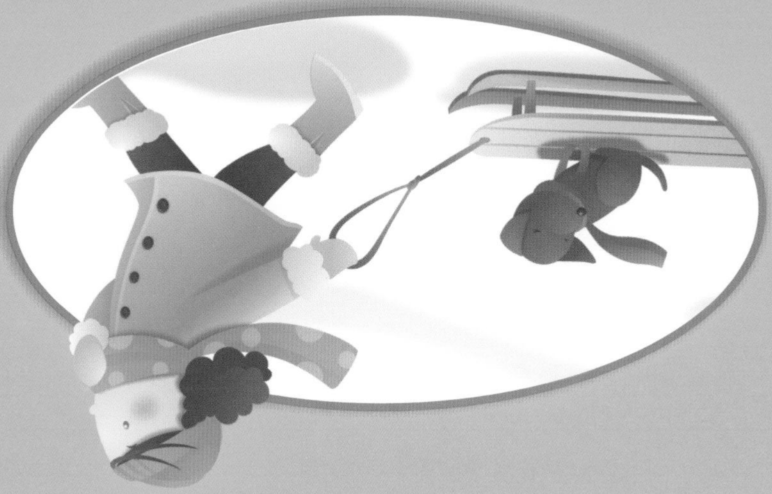

Synonyms

Answer Key

(fold)

Response Form

Synonyms

Draw lines to match the three synonyms.

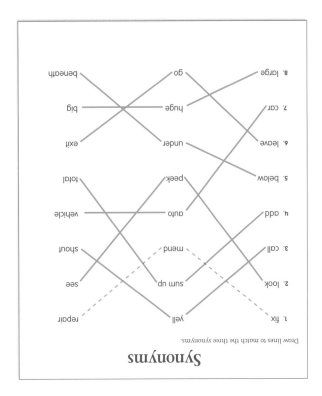

1. fix	yell	repair
2. look	sum up	see
3. call	mend	shout
4. add	auto	vehicle
5. below	peek	total
6. leave	under	exit
7. car	huge	big
8. large	go	beneath

Answer Key

Synonyms

A

Center Mat A — Synonyms

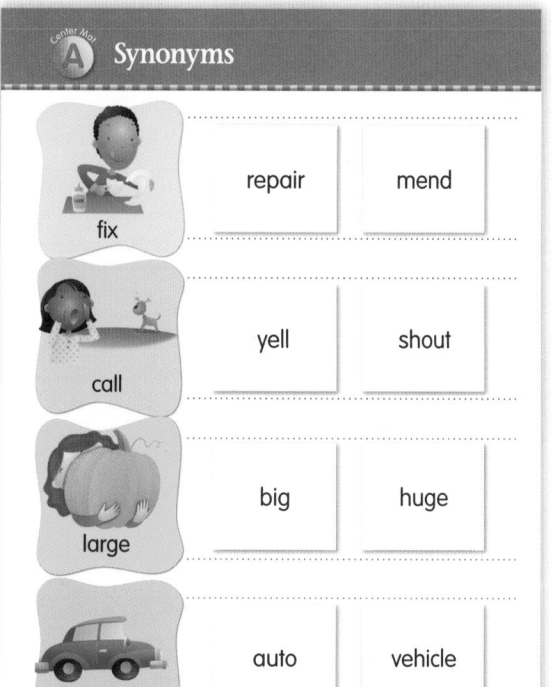

 fix	repair	mend
 call	yell	shout
 large	big	huge
 car	auto	vehicle

B

Center Mat B — Synonyms

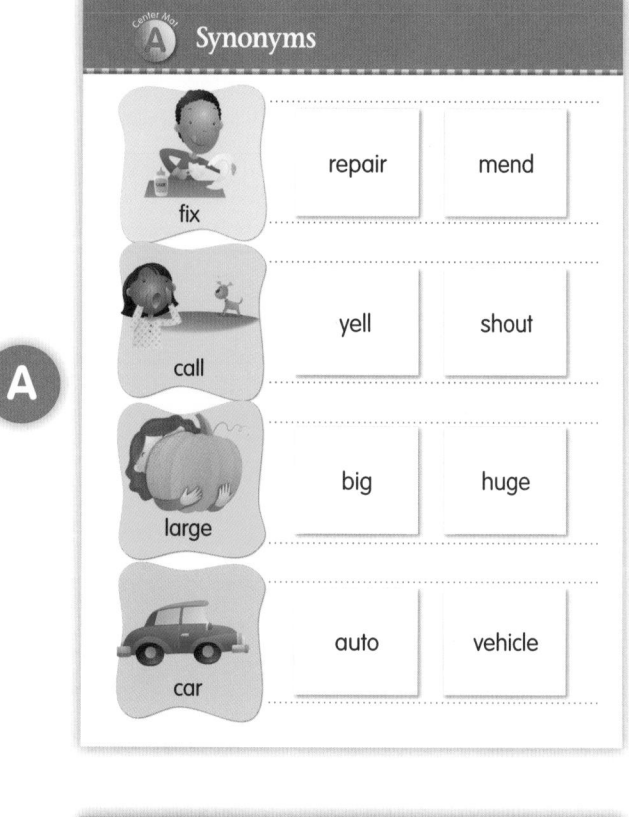

 look	peek	see
 add	total	sum up
 below	under	beneath
 leave	go	exit

Center Mat A

Synonyms

fix

call

large

car

Center Mat B

Synonyms

look

add

below

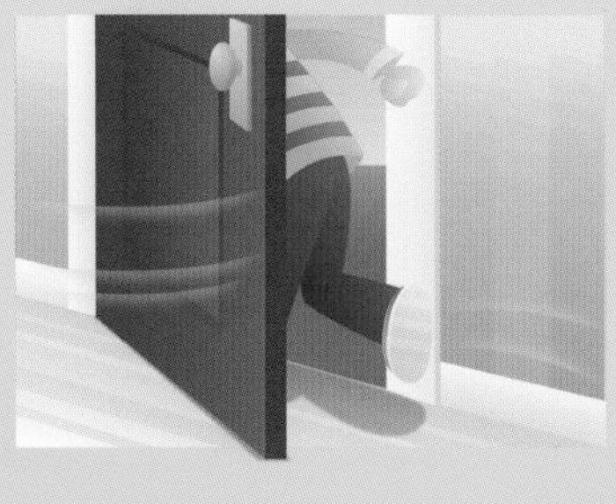

leave

repair	mend	yell	shout
big	huge	auto	vehicle
peek	see	total	sum up
under	beneath	go	exit

Synonyms

Take It to Your Seat Centers
Reading & Language
EMC 2842 • © Evan-Moor Corp.

Synonyms

Take It to Your Seat Centers
Reading & Language
EMC 2842 • © Evan-Moor Corp.

Synonyms

Take It to Your Seat Centers
Reading & Language
EMC 2842 • © Evan-Moor Corp.

Synonyms

Take It to Your Seat Centers
Reading & Language
EMC 2842 • © Evan-Moor Corp.

Synonyms

Take It to Your Seat Centers
Reading & Language
EMC 2842 • © Evan-Moor Corp.

Synonyms

Take It to Your Seat Centers
Reading & Language
EMC 2842 • © Evan-Moor Corp.

Synonyms

Take It to Your Seat Centers
Reading & Language
EMC 2842 • © Evan-Moor Corp.

Synonyms

Take It to Your Seat Centers
Reading & Language
EMC 2842 • © Evan-Moor Corp.

Synonyms

Take It to Your Seat Centers
Reading & Language
EMC 2842 • © Evan-Moor Corp.

Synonyms

Take It to Your Seat Centers
Reading & Language
EMC 2842 • © Evan-Moor Corp.

Synonyms

Take It to Your Seat Centers
Reading & Language
EMC 2842 • © Evan-Moor Corp.

Synonyms

Take It to Your Seat Centers
Reading & Language
EMC 2842 • © Evan-Moor Corp.

Synonyms

Take It to Your Seat Centers
Reading & Language
EMC 2842 • © Evan-Moor Corp.

Synonyms

Take It to Your Seat Centers
Reading & Language
EMC 2842 • © Evan-Moor Corp.

Synonyms

Take It to Your Seat Centers
Reading & Language
EMC 2842 • © Evan-Moor Corp.

Synonyms

Take It to Your Seat Centers
Reading & Language
EMC 2842 • © Evan-Moor Corp.

Take It to Your Seat Centers

Antonyms

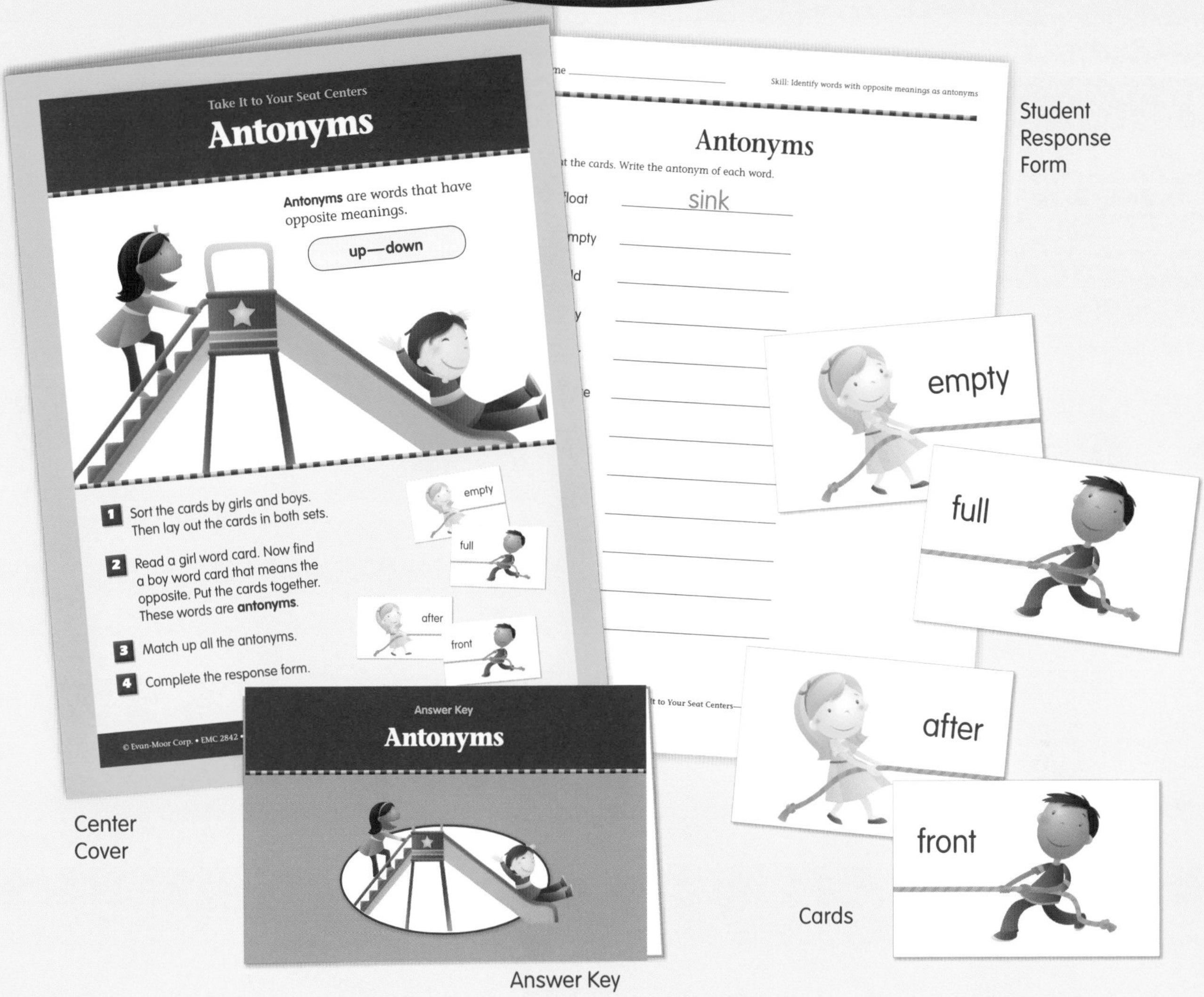

Skill
Identify words with opposite meanings as antonyms

Prepare the Center
Follow the directions on page 3.

Introduce the Center
Demonstrate how to use the center. State the goal:
You will match word cards that mean the opposite of each other.

Name ______________________

Skill: Identify words with opposite meanings as antonyms

Antonyms

Look at the cards. Write the antonym of each word.

1. float ______sink______
2. empty ____________
3. add ____________
4. dirty ____________
5. after ____________
6. awake ____________
7. open ____________
8. back ____________
9. old ____________
10. short ____________
11. broken ____________
12. boy ____________

Antonyms

Antonyms are words that have opposite meanings.

up—down

1. Sort the cards by girls and boys. Then lay out the cards in both sets.
2. Read a girl word card. Now find a boy word card that means the opposite. Put the cards together. These words are **antonyms**.
3. Match up all the antonyms.
4. Complete the response form.

Antonyms

Answer Key

(fold)

Antonyms

Look at the cards. Write the antonym of each word.

1. float sink
2. empty full
3. add subtract
4. dirty clean
5. after before
6. awake asleep
7. open closed
8. back front
9. old new
10. short long
11. broken fixed
12. boy girl

Answer Key

Antonyms

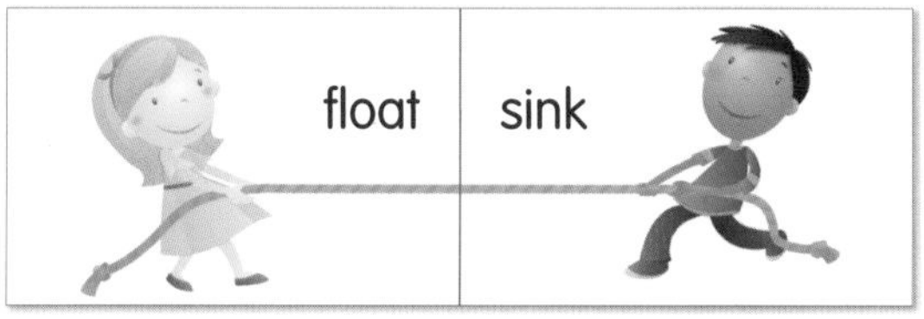

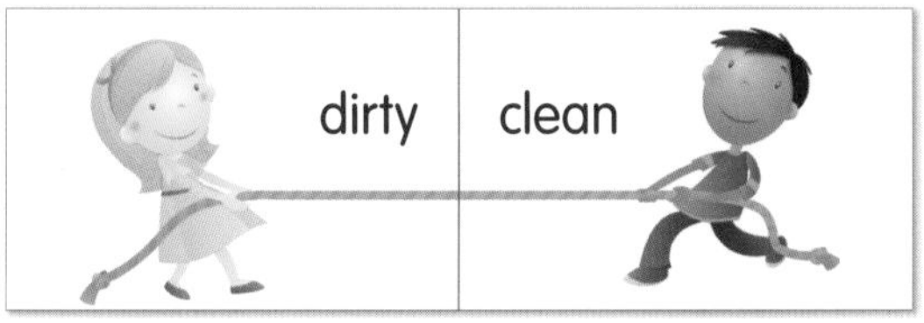

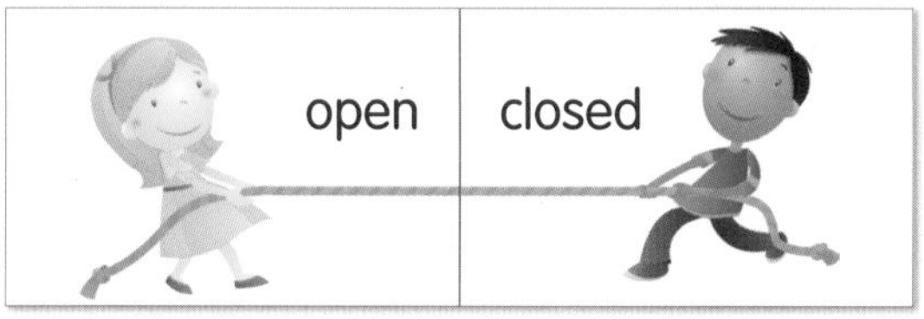

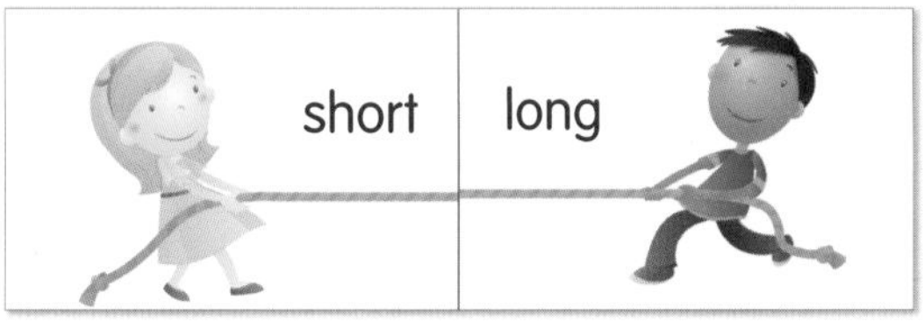

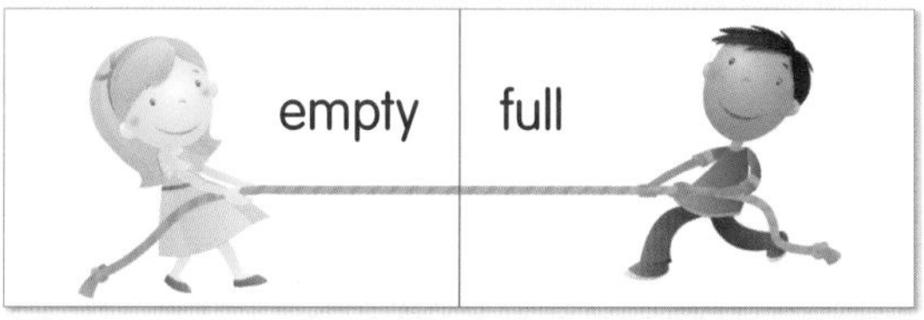

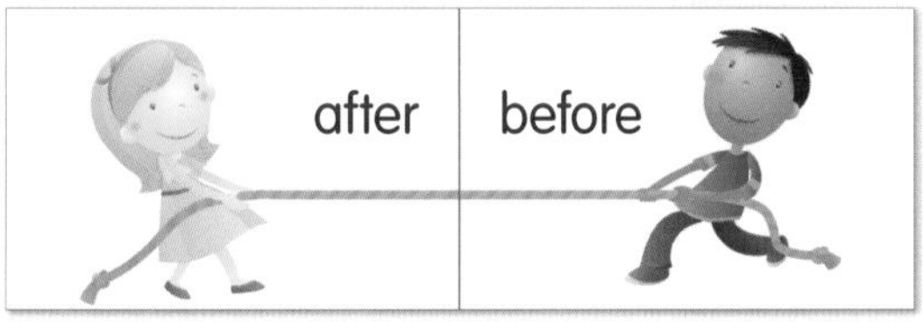

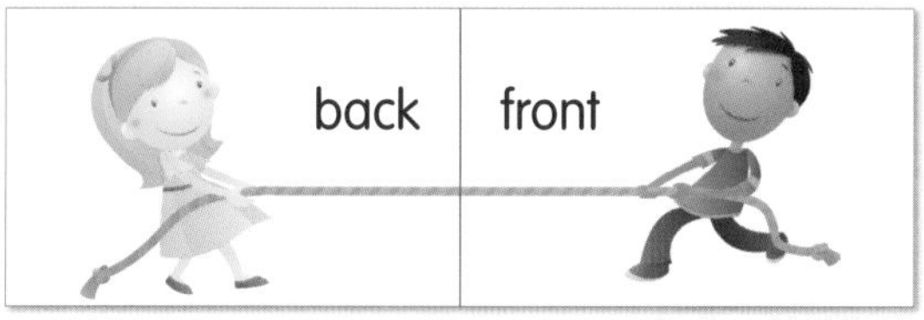

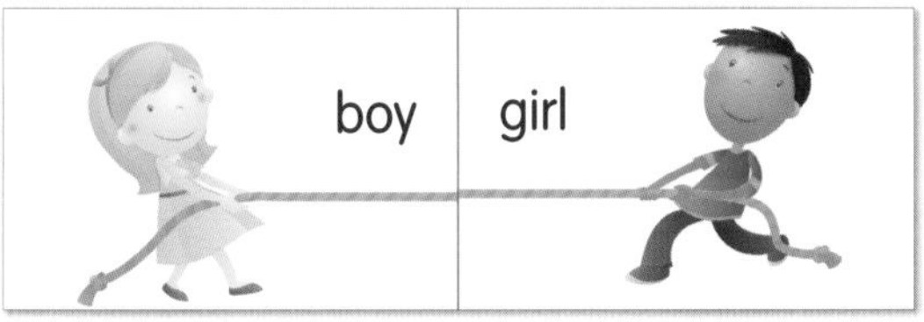

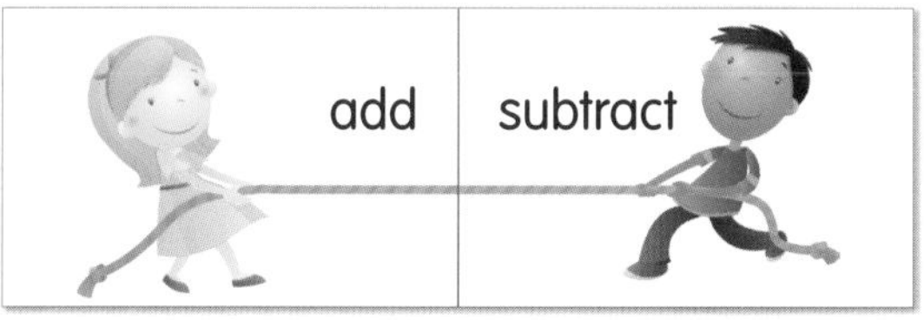

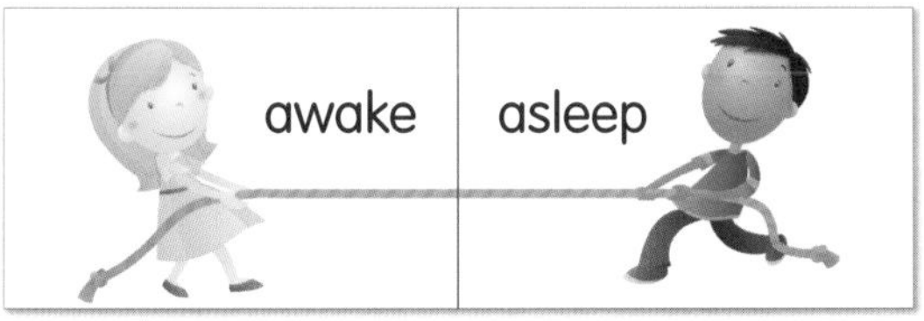

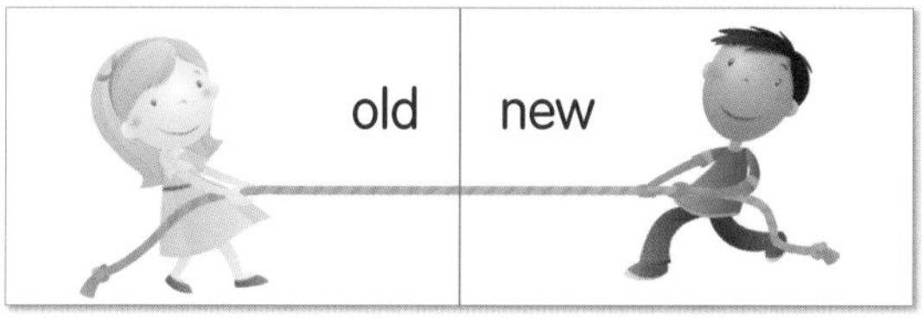

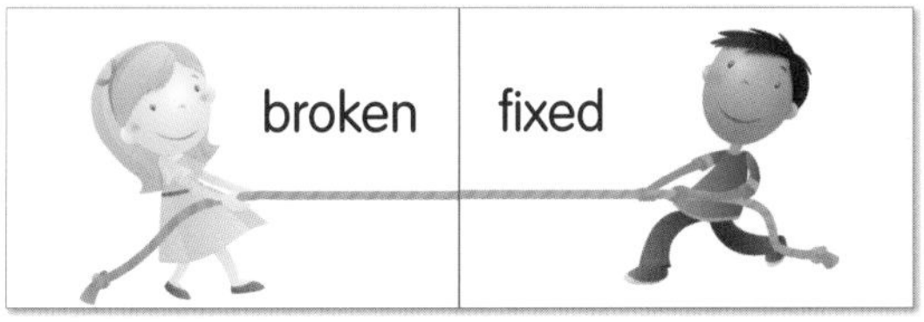

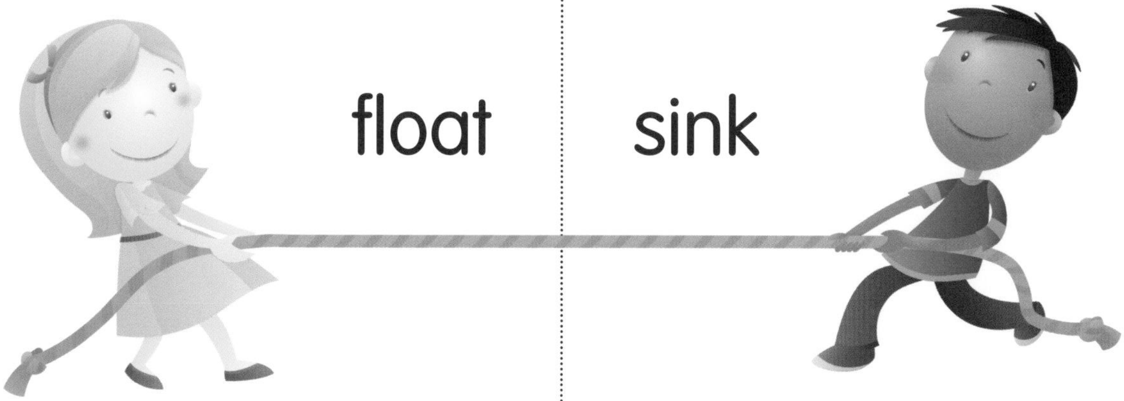

float

sink

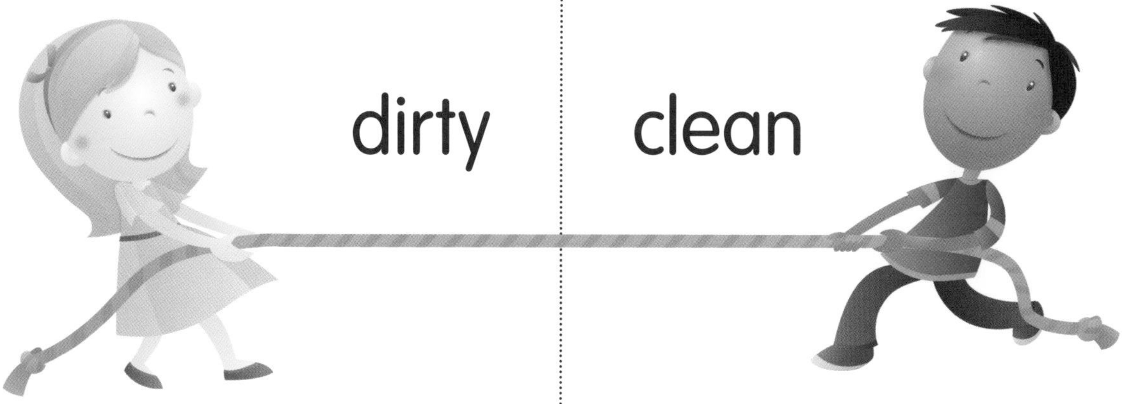

dirty

clean

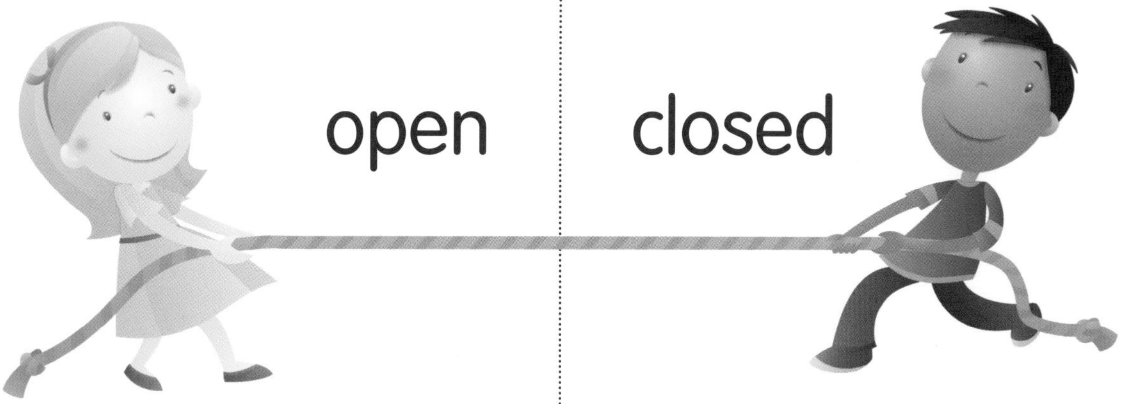

open

closed

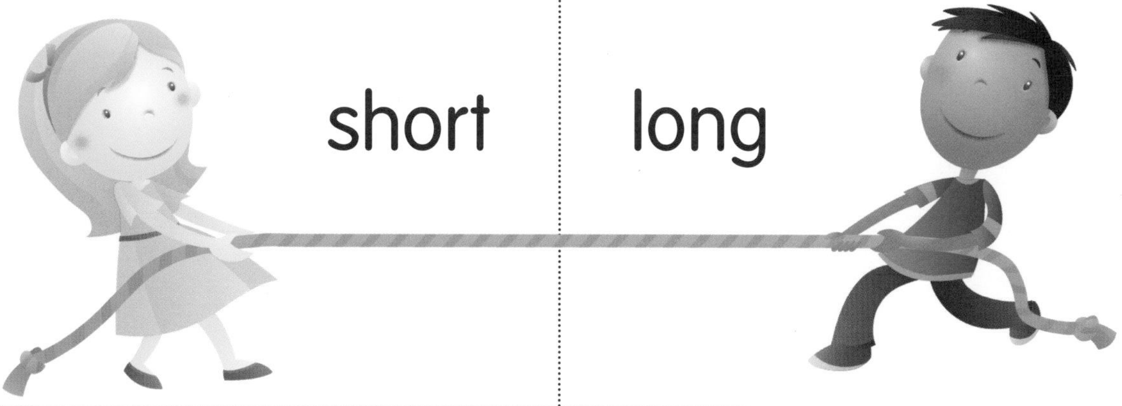

short

long

Antonyms

Take It to Your Seat Centers
Reading & Language
EMC 2842 • © Evan-Moor Corp.

Antonyms

Take It to Your Seat Centers
Reading & Language
EMC 2842 • © Evan-Moor Corp.

Antonyms

Take It to Your Seat Centers
Reading & Language
EMC 2842 • © Evan-Moor Corp.

Antonyms

Take It to Your Seat Centers
Reading & Language
EMC 2842 • © Evan-Moor Corp.

Antonyms

Take It to Your Seat Centers
Reading & Language
EMC 2842 • © Evan-Moor Corp.

Antonyms

Take It to Your Seat Centers
Reading & Language
EMC 2842 • © Evan-Moor Corp.

Antonyms

Take It to Your Seat Centers
Reading & Language
EMC 2842 • © Evan-Moor Corp.

Antonyms

Take It to Your Seat Centers
Reading & Language
EMC 2842 • © Evan-Moor Corp.

empty

full

after

before

back

front

boy

girl

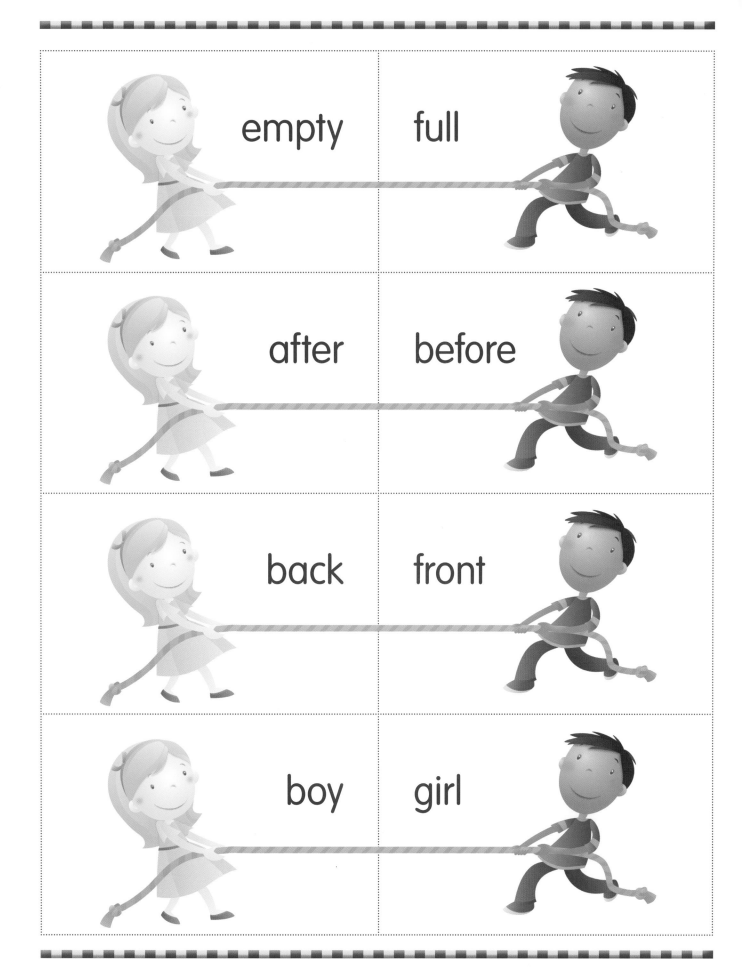

Antonyms

Take It to Your Seat Centers
Reading & Language
EMC 2842 • © Evan-Moor Corp.

Antonyms

Take It to Your Seat Centers
Reading & Language
EMC 2842 • © Evan-Moor Corp.

Antonyms

Take It to Your Seat Centers
Reading & Language
EMC 2842 • © Evan-Moor Corp.

Antonyms

Take It to Your Seat Centers
Reading & Language
EMC 2842 • © Evan-Moor Corp.

Antonyms

Take It to Your Seat Centers
Reading & Language
EMC 2842 • © Evan-Moor Corp.

Antonyms

Take It to Your Seat Centers
Reading & Language
EMC 2842 • © Evan-Moor Corp.

Antonyms

Take It to Your Seat Centers
Reading & Language
EMC 2842 • © Evan-Moor Corp.

Antonyms

Take It to Your Seat Centers
Reading & Language
EMC 2842 • © Evan-Moor Corp.

add

subtract

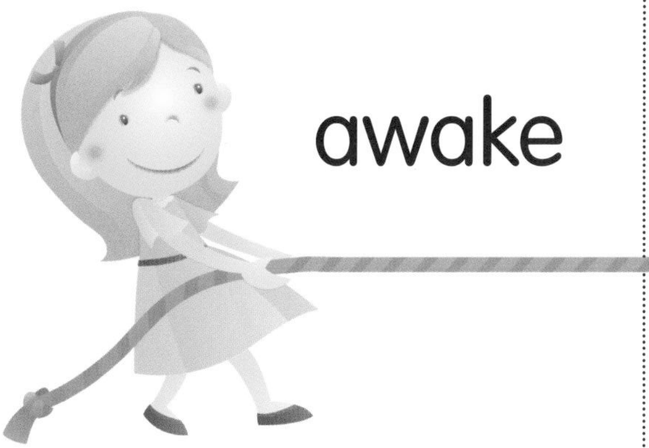

awake

asleep

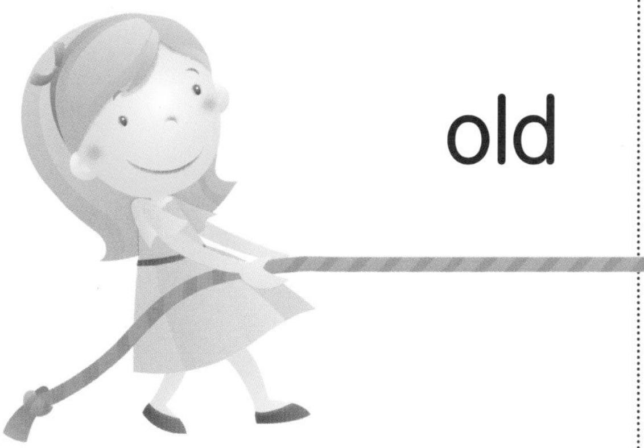

old

new

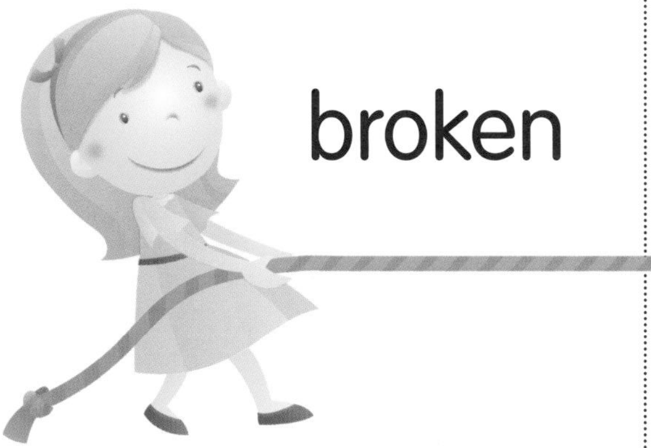

broken

fixed

Antonyms

Take It to Your Seat Centers
Reading & Language
EMC 2842 • © Evan-Moor Corp.

Antonyms

Take It to Your Seat Centers
Reading & Language
EMC 2842 • © Evan-Moor Corp.

Antonyms

Take It to Your Seat Centers
Reading & Language
EMC 2842 • © Evan-Moor Corp.

Antonyms

Take It to Your Seat Centers
Reading & Language
EMC 2842 • © Evan-Moor Corp.

Antonyms

Take It to Your Seat Centers
Reading & Language
EMC 2842 • © Evan-Moor Corp.

Antonyms

Take It to Your Seat Centers
Reading & Language
EMC 2842 • © Evan-Moor Corp.

Antonyms

Take It to Your Seat Centers
Reading & Language
EMC 2842 • © Evan-Moor Corp.

Antonyms

Take It to Your Seat Centers
Reading & Language
EMC 2842 • © Evan-Moor Corp.

Take It to Your Seat Centers

Homophones

Skill
Identify the correct homophone to use in a sentence

Prepare the Center
Follow the directions on page 3.

Introduce the Center
Demonstrate how to use the center. State the goal: *You will find the correct homophone to complete each sentence.*

Name ______________________ Skill: Identify the correct homophone to use in a sentence

Homophones

Look at the mats. Write the word you used to complete each sentence on the line. Then write the homophone you did not use in the box.

1. My favorite aunt is visiting this summer. [ant]
2. I ____________ my library book all afternoon. [ ]
3. Did you ____________ the colorful rainbow in the sky? [ ]
4. I brush my ____________ before going to bed. [ ]
5. Dad picked a ____________ in the garden just for me. [ ]
6. Tim saw a huge grizzly ____________ at the zoo. [ ]
7. Kai found a hole in his left ____________ after the hike. [ ]
8. Carlos quickly ____________ out the candles on his cake. [ ]
9. A family of ____________ ran through the woods at dusk. [ ]
10. Mom will help me ____________ up the rip in my pants. [ ]
11. The cowboy guided the ____________ of cattle. [ ]
12. How much ____________ did you put in the campfire? [ ]

Homophones

Homophones are two words that sound the same but are spelled differently.

see sea : ant aunt

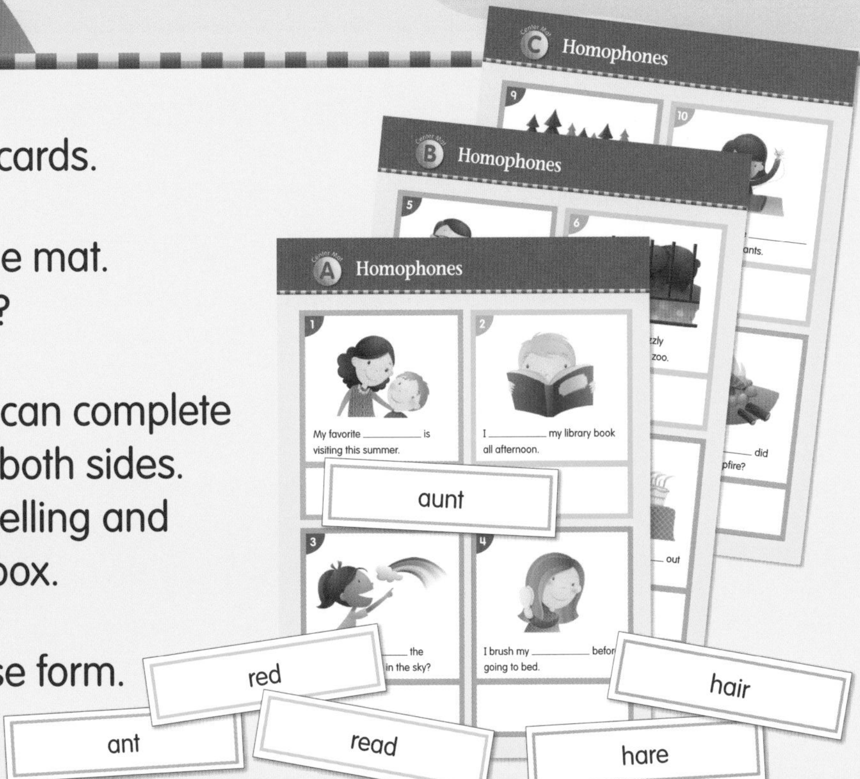

1. Lay out the mats and cards.
2. Read sentence 1 on the mat. What word is missing?
3. Find a word card that can complete the sentence. Look at both sides. Choose the correct spelling and place the card in the box.
4. Complete the response form.

Homophones

Answer Key

(fold)

Homophones

Look at the mats. Write the word you used to complete each sentence on the line.
Then write the homophone you did not use in the box.

1. My favorite **aunt** is visiting this summer. — ant
2. I **read** my library book all afternoon. — red
3. Did you **see** the colorful rainbow in the sky? — sea
4. I brush my **hair** before going to bed. — hare
5. Dad picked a **flower** in the garden just for me. — flour
6. Tim saw a huge grizzly **bear** at the zoo. — bare
7. Kai found a hole in his left **shoe** after the hike. — shoo
8. Carlos quickly **blew** out the candles on his cake. — blue
9. A family of **deer** ran through the woods at dusk. — dear
10. Mom will help me **sew** up the rip in my pants. — so
11. The cowboy guided the **herd** of cattle. — heard
12. How much **wood** did you put in the campfire? — would

Answer Key

Homophones

A

Center Mat A
Homophones
1
My favorite ________ is visiting this summer.
aunt
2
I ________ my library book all afternoon.
read
3
Did you ________ the colorful rainbow in the sky?
see
4
I brush my ________ before going to bed.
hair

B

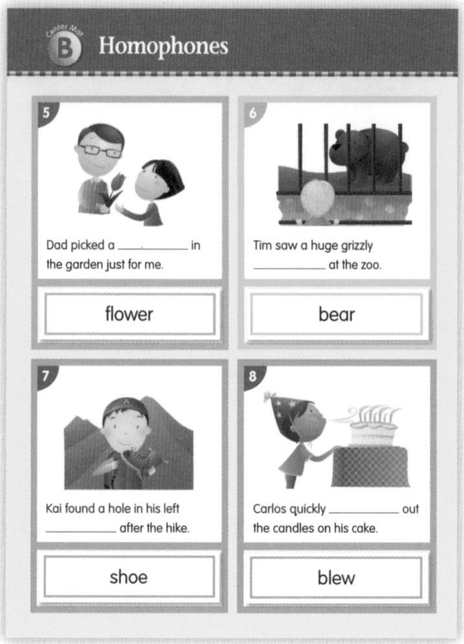
Center Mat B
Homophones
5
Dad picked a ________ in the garden just for me.
flower
6
Tim saw a huge grizzly ________ at the zoo.
bear
7
Kai found a hole in his left ________ after the hike.
shoe
8
Carlos quickly ________ out the candles on his cake.
blew

C

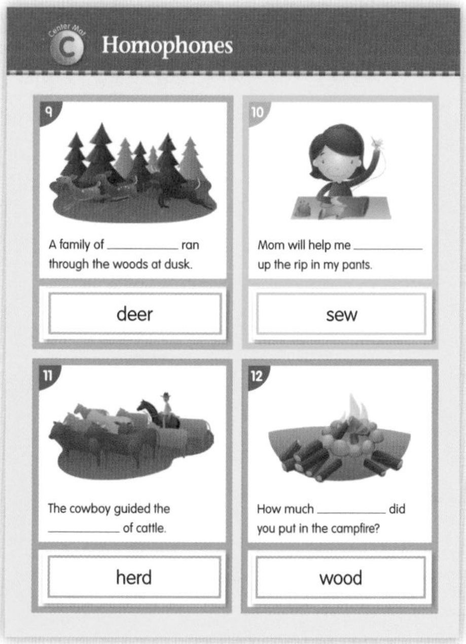
Center Mat C
Homophones
9
A family of ________ ran through the woods at dusk.
deer
10
Mom will help me ________ up the rip in my pants.
sew
11
The cowboy guided the ________ of cattle.
herd
12
How much ________ did you put in the campfire?
wood

Center Mat A

Homophones

1

My favorite ____________ is visiting this summer.

2

I ____________ my library book all afternoon.

3

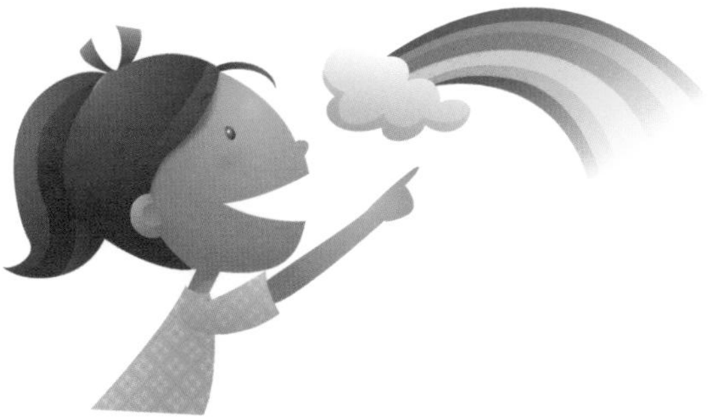

Did you ____________ the colorful rainbow in the sky?

4

I brush my ____________ before going to bed.

Homophones

Center Mat B

5

Dad picked a ____________ in the garden just for me.

6

Tim saw a huge grizzly ____________ at the zoo.

7

Kai found a hole in his left ____________ after the hike.

8

Carlos quickly ____________ out the candles on his cake.

Homophones

9

A family of ____________ ran through the woods at dusk.

10

Mom will help me ____________ up the rip in my pants.

11

The cowboy guided the ____________ of cattle.

12

How much ____________ did you put in the campfire?

aunt	read
see	hair
flower	bear
shoe	blew
deer	sew
herd	wood

red	ant
hare	sea
bare	flour
blue	shoo
so	dear
would	heard

Fantasy or Reality?

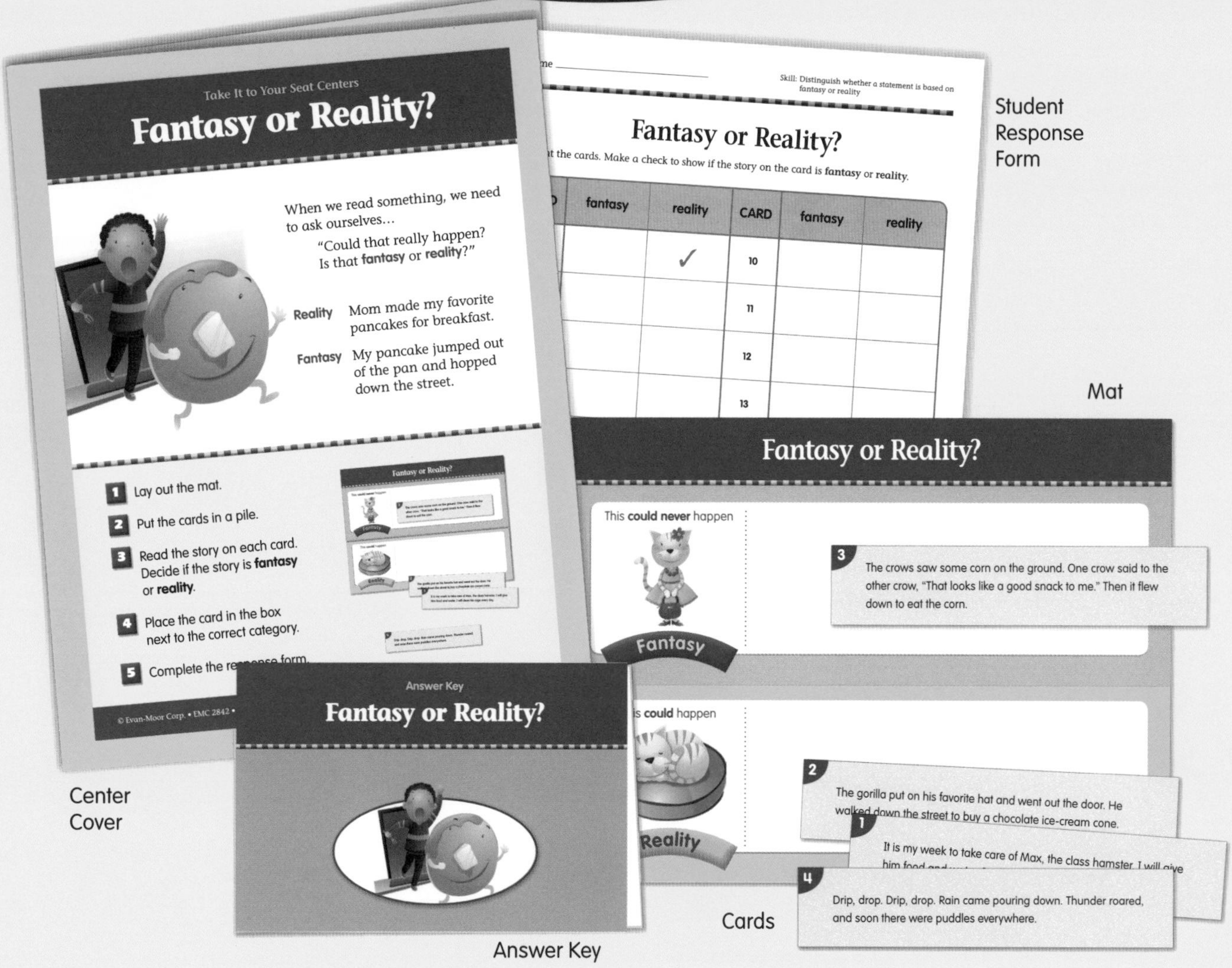

Skill
Distinguish whether a statement is based on fantasy or reality

Prepare the Center
Follow the directions on page 3.

Introduce the Center
Demonstrate how to use the center. State the goal: *You will read stories and then decide if they are reality or fantasy.*

Name ______________________

Skill: Distinguish whether a statement is based on fantasy or reality

Fantasy or Reality?

Look at the cards. Make a check to show if the story on the card is **fantasy** or **reality**.

CARD	fantasy	reality	CARD	fantasy	reality
1		✓	10		
2			11		
3			12		
4			13		
5			14		
6			15		
7			16		
8			17		
9			18		

Fantasy or Reality?

When we read something, we need to ask ourselves...

"Could that really happen? Is that **fantasy** or **reality**?"

Reality Mom made my favorite pancakes for breakfast.

Fantasy My pancake jumped out of the pan and hopped down the street.

1. Lay out the mat.
2. Put the cards in a pile.
3. Read the story on each card. Decide if the story is **fantasy** or **reality**.
4. Place the card in the box next to the correct category.
5. Complete the response form.

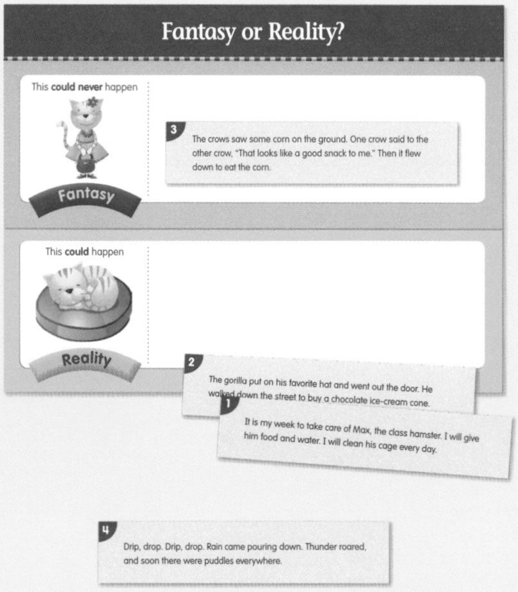

Answer Key

Fantasy or Reality?

(fold)

Response Form

Fantasy or Reality?

Look at the cards. Make a check to show if the story on the card is **fantasy** or **reality**.

CARD	fantasy	reality	CARD	fantasy	reality
1		✓	10		✓
2	✓		11	✓	
3	✓		12		✓
4		✓	13	✓	
5		✓	14	✓	
6	✓		15		✓
7		✓	16	✓	
8	✓		17		✓
9	✓		18		✓

Answer Key

Fantasy or Reality?

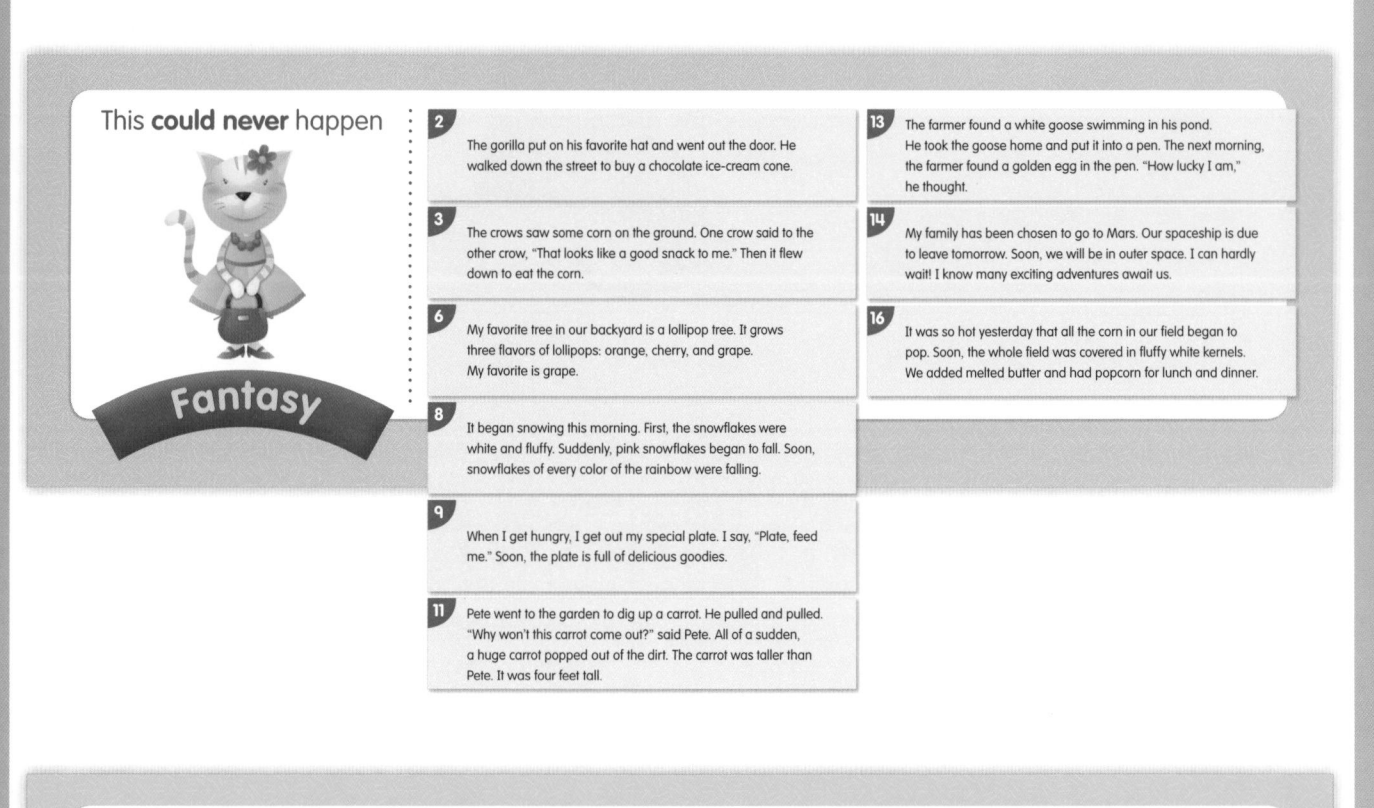

This **could never** happen

2 The gorilla put on his favorite hat and went out the door. He walked down the street to buy a chocolate ice-cream cone.

3 The crows saw some corn on the ground. One crow said to the other crow, "That looks like a good snack to me." Then it flew down to eat the corn.

6 My favorite tree in our backyard is a lollipop tree. It grows three flavors of lollipops: orange, cherry, and grape. My favorite is grape.

8 It began snowing this morning. First, the snowflakes were white and fluffy. Suddenly, pink snowflakes began to fall. Soon, snowflakes of every color of the rainbow were falling.

9 When I get hungry, I get out my special plate. I say, "Plate, feed me." Soon, the plate is full of delicious goodies.

11 Pete went to the garden to dig up a carrot. He pulled and pulled. "Why won't this carrot come out?" said Pete. All of a sudden, a huge carrot popped out of the dirt. The carrot was taller than Pete. It was four feet tall.

13 The farmer found a white goose swimming in his pond. He took the goose home and put it into a pen. The next morning, the farmer found a golden egg in the pen. "How lucky I am," he thought.

14 My family has been chosen to go to Mars. Our spaceship is due to leave tomorrow. Soon, we will be in outer space. I can hardly wait! I know many exciting adventures await us.

16 It was so hot yesterday that all the corn in our field began to pop. Soon, the whole field was covered in fluffy white kernels. We added melted butter and had popcorn for lunch and dinner.

This **could** happen

1 It is my week to take care of Max, the class hamster. I will give him food and water. I will clean his cage every day.

4 Drip, drop. Drip, drop. Rain came pouring down. Thunder roared, and soon there were puddles everywhere.

5 Butter was a small, fluffy hen. She was as yellow as a cube of butter. That is how she got her name. Almost every day, Butter laid an egg in her nest.

7 Bees buzz around flowers. They are busy collecting nectar to take back to their hive. The bees use the nectar to make honey.

10 A little gray mouse lives in the wall of my kitchen. The mouse only comes out when I am gone. The mouse looks for food to nibble on. If I come back, the mouse hides in its hole.

12 Bats have wings and they can fly, but they are not birds. Bats' wings are covered in skin. Birds' wings are covered with feathers.

15 One morning, Mary saw blackbirds eating the beans in her garden. She grabbed a pan and a big spoon. She banged on the pan with the spoon. Bang! Bang! Soon, all the blackbirds were gone!

17 What is black and white and looks like a big bear? A giant panda! There are very few giant pandas left in the world. In the wild, they live in bamboo forests. These forests are found only in parts of China.

18 Kim put her letter inside the mailbox. The letter was for her best friend, Maggie. Kim wanted to know if Maggie could come for a visit. Kim can't wait to find out if Maggie can visit.

Fantasy or Reality?

This **could never** happen

Fantasy

This **could** happen

Reality

1

It is my week to take care of Max, the class hamster. I will give him food and water. I will clean his cage every day.

2

The gorilla put on his favorite hat and went out the door. He walked down the street to buy a chocolate ice-cream cone.

3

The crows saw some corn on the ground. One crow said to the other crow, "That looks like a good snack to me." Then it flew down to eat the corn.

4

Drip, drop. Drip, drop. Rain came pouring down. Thunder roared, and soon there were puddles everywhere.

5

Butter was a small, fluffy hen. She was as yellow as a cube of butter. That is how she got her name. Almost every day, Butter laid an egg in her nest.

6

My favorite tree in our backyard is a lollipop tree. It grows three flavors of lollipops: orange, cherry, and grape.
My favorite is grape.

Fantasy or Reality?

Take It to Your Seat Centers
Reading & Language
EMC 2842 • © Evan-Moor Corp.

Fantasy or Reality?

Take It to Your Seat Centers
Reading & Language
EMC 2842 • © Evan-Moor Corp.

Fantasy or Reality?

Take It to Your Seat Centers
Reading & Language
EMC 2842 • © Evan-Moor Corp.

Fantasy or Reality?

Take It to Your Seat Centers
Reading & Language
EMC 2842 • © Evan-Moor Corp.

Fantasy or Reality?

Take It to Your Seat Centers
Reading & Language
EMC 2842 • © Evan-Moor Corp.

Fantasy or Reality?

Take It to Your Seat Centers
Reading & Language
EMC 2842 • © Evan-Moor Corp.

7

Bees buzz around flowers. They are busy collecting nectar to take back to their hive. The bees use the nectar to make honey.

8

It began snowing this morning. First, the snowflakes were white and fluffy. Suddenly, pink snowflakes began to fall. Soon, snowflakes of every color of the rainbow were falling.

9

When I get hungry, I get out my special plate. I say, "Plate, feed me." Soon, the plate is full of delicious goodies.

10

A little gray mouse lives in the wall of my kitchen. The mouse only comes out when I am gone. The mouse looks for food to nibble on. If I come back, the mouse hides in its hole.

11

Pete went to the garden to dig up a carrot. He pulled and pulled. "Why won't this carrot come out?" said Pete. All of a sudden, a huge carrot popped out of the dirt. The carrot was taller than Pete. It was four feet tall.

12

Bats have wings and they can fly, but they are not birds. Bats' wings are covered in skin. Birds' wings are covered with feathers.

Fantasy or Reality?

Take It to Your Seat Centers
Reading & Language
EMC 2842 • © Evan-Moor Corp.

Fantasy or Reality?

Take It to Your Seat Centers
Reading & Language
EMC 2842 • © Evan-Moor Corp.

Fantasy or Reality?

Take It to Your Seat Centers
Reading & Language
EMC 2842 • © Evan-Moor Corp.

Fantasy or Reality?

Take It to Your Seat Centers
Reading & Language
EMC 2842 • © Evan-Moor Corp.

Fantasy or Reality?

Take It to Your Seat Centers
Reading & Language
EMC 2842 • © Evan-Moor Corp.

Fantasy or Reality?

Take It to Your Seat Centers
Reading & Language
EMC 2842 • © Evan-Moor Corp.

13 The farmer found a white goose swimming in his pond. He took the goose home and put it into a pen. The next morning, the farmer found a golden egg in the pen. "How lucky I am," he thought.

14 My family has been chosen to go to Mars. Our spaceship is due to leave tomorrow. Soon, we will be in outer space. I can hardly wait! I know many exciting adventures await us.

15 One morning, Mary saw blackbirds eating the beans in her garden. She grabbed a pan and a big spoon. She banged on the pan with the spoon. Bang! Bang! Soon, all the blackbirds were gone!

16 It was so hot yesterday that all the corn in our field began to pop. Soon, the whole field was covered in fluffy white kernels. We added melted butter and had popcorn for lunch and dinner.

17 What is black and white and looks like a big bear? A giant panda! There are very few giant pandas left in the world. In the wild, they live in bamboo forests. These forests are found only in parts of China.

18 Kim put her letter inside the mailbox. The letter was for her best friend, Maggie. Kim wanted to know if Maggie could come for a visit. Kim can't wait to find out if Maggie can visit.

Fantasy or Reality?

Take It to Your Seat Centers
Reading & Language
EMC 2842 • © Evan-Moor Corp.

Fantasy or Reality?

Take It to Your Seat Centers
Reading & Language
EMC 2842 • © Evan-Moor Corp.

Fantasy or Reality?

Take It to Your Seat Centers
Reading & Language
EMC 2842 • © Evan-Moor Corp.

Fantasy or Reality?

Take It to Your Seat Centers
Reading & Language
EMC 2842 • © Evan-Moor Corp.

Fantasy or Reality?

Take It to Your Seat Centers
Reading & Language
EMC 2842 • © Evan-Moor Corp.

Fantasy or Reality?

Take It to Your Seat Centers
Reading & Language
EMC 2842 • © Evan-Moor Corp.

Sequencing

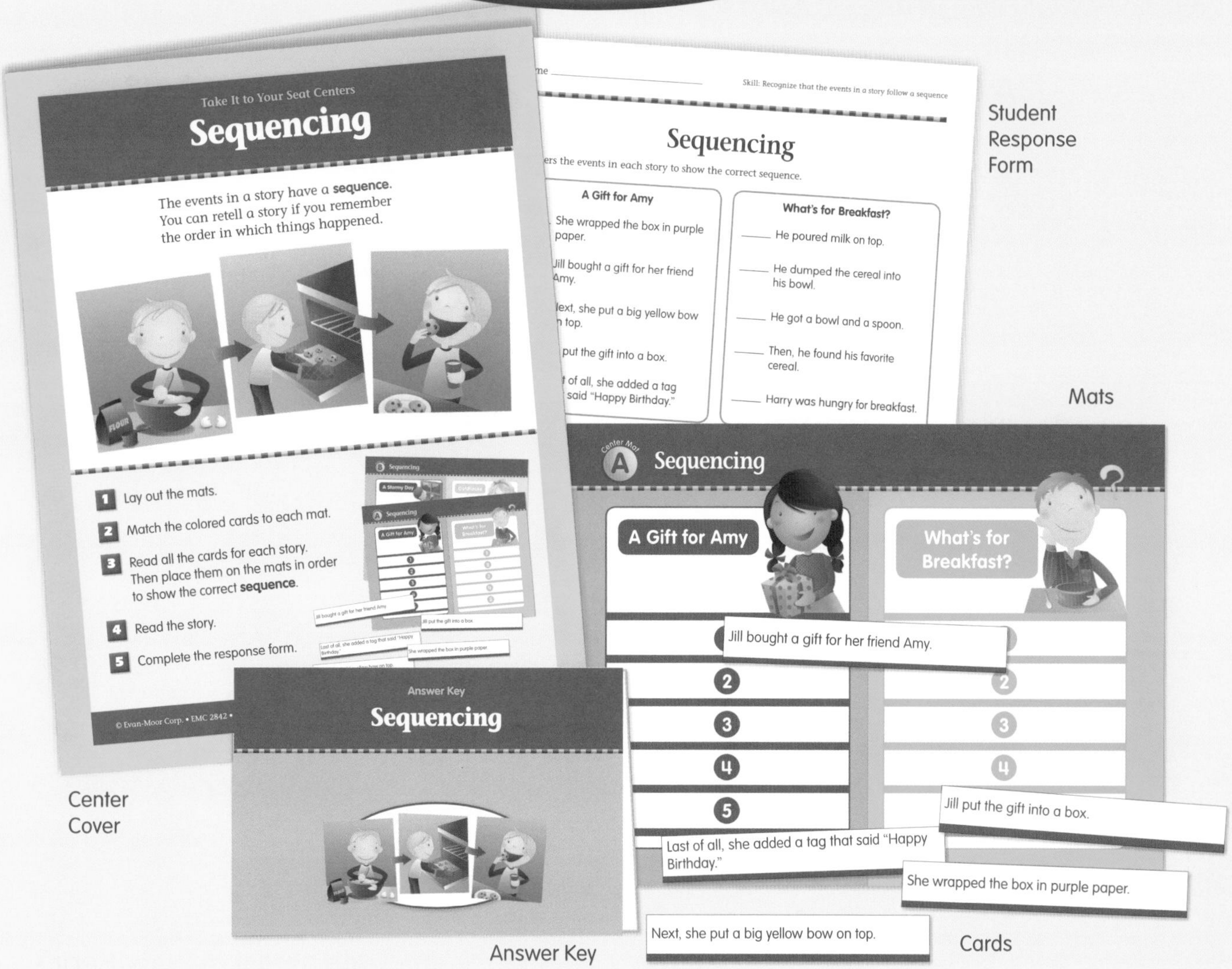

Skill
Recognize that the events in a story follow a sequence

Prepare the Center
Follow the directions on page 3.

Introduce the Center
Demonstrate how to use the center. State the goal: *You will listen for clues as you read stories and then sequence the events.*

Name ______________________ Skill: Recognize that the events in a story follow a sequence

Sequencing

Numbers the events in each story to show the correct sequence.

A Gift for Amy

_____ She wrapped the box in purple paper.

__1__ Jill bought a gift for her friend Amy.

_____ Next, she put a big yellow bow on top.

_____ Jill put the gift into a box.

_____ Last of all, she added a tag that said "Happy Birthday."

What's for Breakfast?

_____ He poured milk on top.

_____ He dumped the cereal into his bowl.

_____ He got a bowl and a spoon.

_____ Then, he found his favorite cereal.

_____ Harry was hungry for breakfast.

A Stormy Day

_____ "Wow, it is starting to pour," he said.

_____ He was ready for the puddles!

_____ He slipped on his new yellow slicker.

_____ Sam looked out the window and saw big black clouds.

_____ Then, he put on his big red rainboots.

Goldilocks

_____ Goldi went into the Bears' house while they were away.

_____ Second, she sat in Baby Bear's chair and broke it.

_____ Goldi was shocked when she woke up and saw the bears. She ran home and never came back.

_____ Then, she went to sleep in Baby Bear's bed.

_____ First, she ate all of Baby Bear's porridge.

Sequencing

The events in a story have a **sequence**. You can retell a story if you remember the order in which things happened.

1. Lay out the mats.
2. Match the colored cards to each mat.
3. Read all the cards for each story. Then place them on the mats in order to show the correct **sequence**.
4. Read the story.
5. Complete the response form.

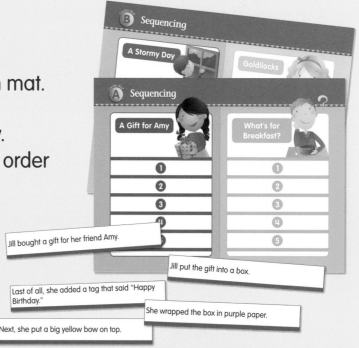

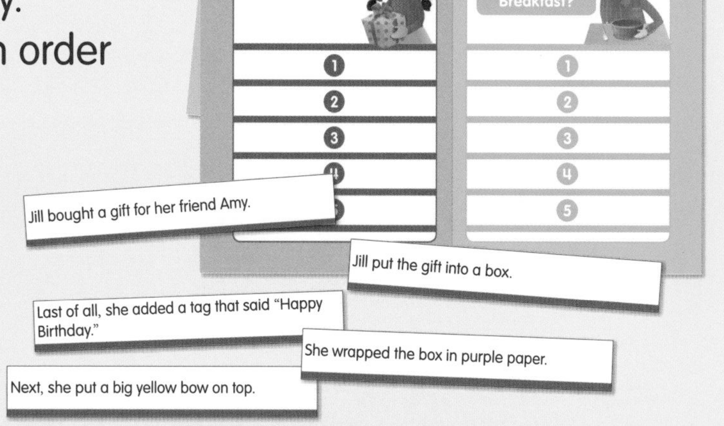

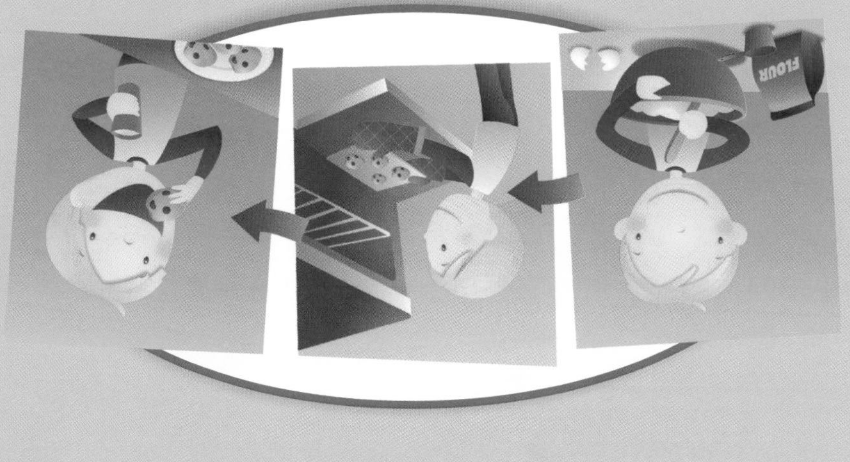

Sequencing

Answer Key

(fold)

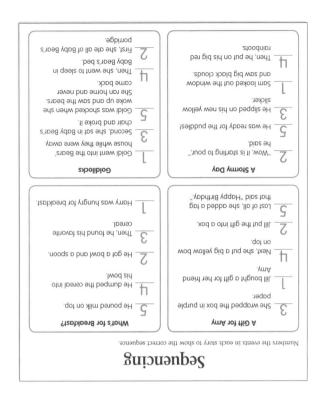

Response Form

Sequencing

Numbers the events in each story to show the correct sequence.

A Gift for Amy

3 She wrapped the box in purple paper.

1 Jill bought a gift for her friend Amy.

4 Next, she put a big yellow bow on top.

2 Jill put the gift into a box.

5 Last of all, she added a tag that said "Happy Birthday."

What's for Breakfast?

5 He poured milk on top.

4 He dumped the cereal into his bowl.

2 He got a bowl and a spoon.

3 Then, he found his favorite cereal.

1 Harry was hungry for breakfast.

A Stormy Day

2 "Wow, it is starting to pour," he said.

5 He was ready for the puddles!

3 He slipped on his new yellow slicker.

1 Sam looked out the window and saw big black clouds.

4 Then, he put on his big red rainboots.

Goldilocks

1 Goldi went into the Bears' house while they were away.

3 Second, she sat in Baby Bear's chair and broke it.

5 Goldi was shocked when she woke up and saw the bears. She ran home and never came back.

4 Then, she went to sleep in Baby Bear's bed.

2 First, she ate all of Baby Bear's porridge.

Answer Key

Sequencing

A

Center Mat A — Sequencing

A Gift for Amy

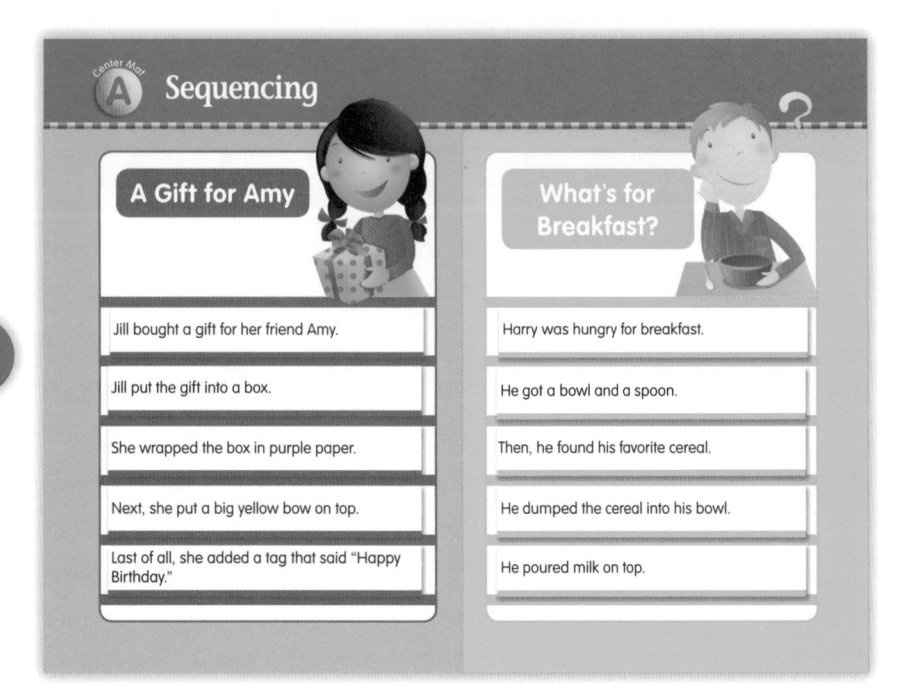

1. Jill bought a gift for her friend Amy.
2. Jill put the gift into a box.
3. She wrapped the box in purple paper.
4. Next, she put a big yellow bow on top.
5. Last of all, she added a tag that said "Happy Birthday."

What's for Breakfast?

1. Harry was hungry for breakfast.
2. He got a bowl and a spoon.
3. Then, he found his favorite cereal.
4. He dumped the cereal into his bowl.
5. He poured milk on top.

B

Center Mat B — Sequencing

A Stormy Day

1. Sam looked out the window and saw big black clouds.
2. "Wow, it is starting to pour," he said.
3. He slipped on his new yellow slicker.
4. Then, he put on his big red rainboots.
5. He was ready for the puddles!

Goldilocks

1. Goldi went into the Bears' house while they were away.
2. First, she ate all of Baby Bear's porridge.
3. Second, she sat in Baby Bear's chair and broke it.
4. Then, she went to sleep in Baby Bear's bed.
5. Goldi was shocked when she woke up and saw the bears. She ran home and never came back.

Center Mat A

Sequencing

A Gift for Amy

1

2

3

4

5

What's for Breakfast?

1

2

3

4

5

Center Mat B

Sequencing

A Stormy Day

1

2

3

4

5

Goldilocks

1

2

3

4

5

Jill bought a gift for her friend Amy.	Harry was hungry for breakfast.
Jill put the gift into a box.	He got a bowl and a spoon.
She wrapped the box in purple paper.	Then, he found his favorite cereal.
Next, she put a big yellow bow on top.	He dumped the cereal into his bowl.
Last of all, she added a tag that said “Happy Birthday.”	He poured milk on top.

Sequencing
Take It to Your Seat Centers—Reading & Language
EMC 2842 • © Evan-Moor Corp.

Sequencing
Take It to Your Seat Centers—Reading & Language
EMC 2842 • © Evan-Moor Corp.

Sequencing
Take It to Your Seat Centers—Reading & Language
EMC 2842 • © Evan-Moor Corp.

Sequencing
Take It to Your Seat Centers—Reading & Language
EMC 2842 • © Evan-Moor Corp.

Sequencing
Take It to Your Seat Centers—Reading & Language
EMC 2842 • © Evan-Moor Corp.

Sequencing
Take It to Your Seat Centers—Reading & Language
EMC 2842 • © Evan-Moor Corp.

Sequencing
Take It to Your Seat Centers—Reading & Language
EMC 2842 • © Evan-Moor Corp.

Sequencing
Take It to Your Seat Centers—Reading & Language
EMC 2842 • © Evan-Moor Corp.

Sequencing
Take It to Your Seat Centers—Reading & Language
EMC 2842 • © Evan-Moor Corp.

Sequencing
Take It to Your Seat Centers—Reading & Language
EMC 2842 • © Evan-Moor Corp.

Goldi went into the Bears' house while they were away.	Sam looked out the window and saw big black clouds.
First, she ate all of Baby Bear's porridge.	"Wow, it is starting to pour," he said.
Second, she sat in Baby Bear's chair and broke it.	He slipped on his new yellow slicker.
Then, she went to sleep in Baby Bear's bed.	Then, he put on his big red rainboots.
Goldi was shocked when she woke up and saw the bears. She ran home and never came back.	He was ready for the puddles!

Sequencing

Take It to Your Seat Centers—Reading & Language
EMC 2842 • © Evan-Moor Corp.

Sequencing

Take It to Your Seat Centers—Reading & Language
EMC 2842 • © Evan-Moor Corp.

Sequencing

Take It to Your Seat Centers—Reading & Language
EMC 2842 • © Evan-Moor Corp.

Sequencing

Take It to Your Seat Centers—Reading & Language
EMC 2842 • © Evan-Moor Corp.

Sequencing

Take It to Your Seat Centers—Reading & Language
EMC 2842 • © Evan-Moor Corp.

Sequencing

Take It to Your Seat Centers—Reading & Language
EMC 2842 • © Evan-Moor Corp.

Sequencing

Take It to Your Seat Centers—Reading & Language
EMC 2842 • © Evan-Moor Corp.

Sequencing

Take It to Your Seat Centers—Reading & Language
EMC 2842 • © Evan-Moor Corp.

Sequencing

Take It to Your Seat Centers—Reading & Language
EMC 2842 • © Evan-Moor Corp.

Sequencing

Take It to Your Seat Centers—Reading & Language
EMC 2842 • © Evan-Moor Corp.

Take It to Your Seat Centers

Predict the Ending

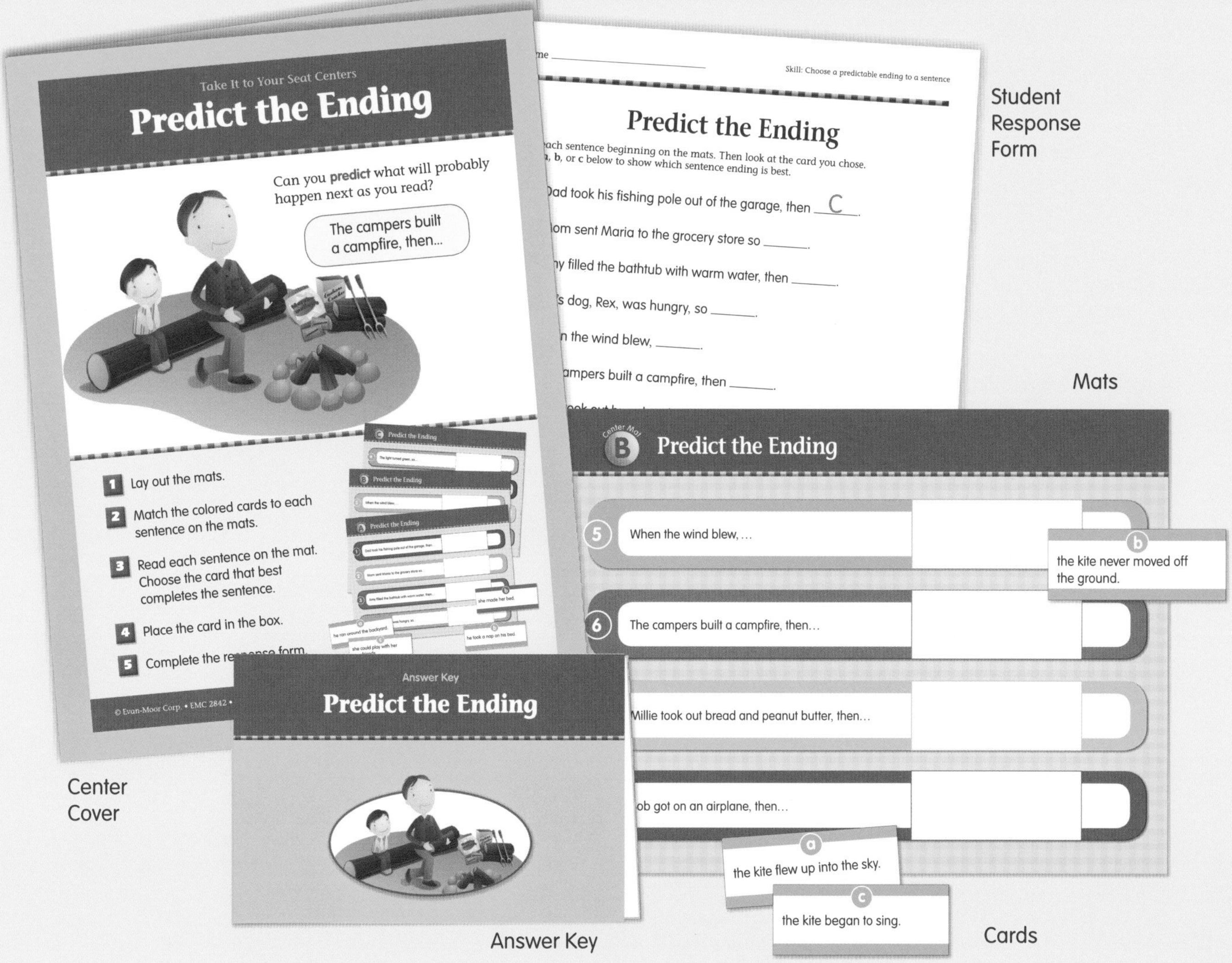

Skill
Choose a predictable ending to a sentence

Prepare the Center
Follow the directions on page 3.

Introduce the Center
Demonstrate how to use the center. State the goal: *You will read the beginnings of sentences and then choose endings that make sense.*

Name ______________________ Skill: Choose a predictable ending to a sentence

Predict the Ending

Read each sentence beginning on the mats. Then look at the card you chose.
Write **a**, **b**, or **c** below to show which sentence ending is best.

1. Dad took his fishing pole out of the garage, then ___C___.
2. Mom sent Maria to the grocery store so ______.
3. Amy filled the bathtub with warm water, then ______.
4. Lee's dog, Rex, was hungry, so ______.
5. When the wind blew, ______.
6. The campers built a campfire, then ______.
7. Millie took out bread and peanut butter, then ______.
8. Bob got on an airplane, then ______.
9. The light turned green, so ______.
10. His bike had a flat tire, so ______.
11. The cat curled up on a chair, and ______.
12. The hen sat on her nest until ______.

Predict the Ending

Can you **predict** what will probably happen next as you read?

The campers built a campfire, then...

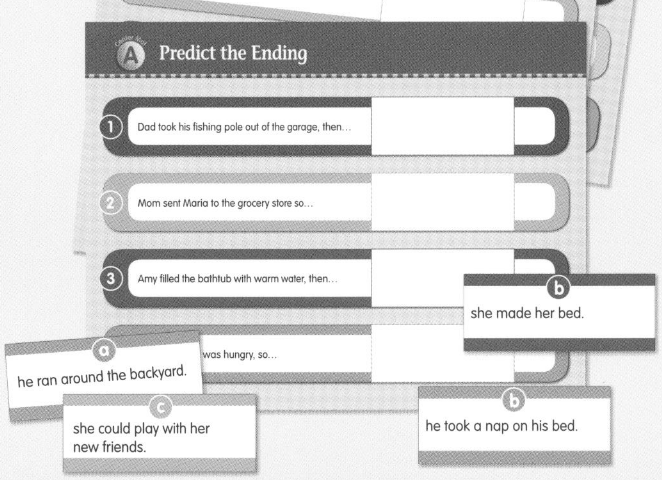

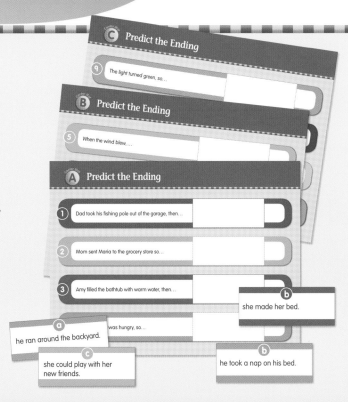

1. Lay out the mats.
2. Match the colored cards to each sentence on the mats.
3. Read each sentence on the mat. Choose the card that best completes the sentence.
4. Place the card in the box.
5. Complete the response form.

Predict the Ending

Answer Key

(fold)

Response Form

Predict the Ending

Read each sentence beginning on the mats. Then look at the card you chose. Write **a**, **b**, or **c** below to show which sentence ending is best.

1. Dad took his fishing pole out of the garage, then c.
2. Mom sent Maria to the grocery store so a.
3. Amy filled the bathtub with warm water, then c.
4. Lee's dog, Rex, was hungry, so c.
5. When the wind blew, a.
6. The campers built a campfire, then a.
7. Millie took out bread and peanut butter, then c.
8. Bob got on an airplane, then b.
9. The light turned green, so b.
10. His bike had a flat tire, so c.
11. The cat curled up on a chair, and a.
12. The hen sat on her nest until c.

Answer Key

Predict the Ending

A

Center Mat A: Predict the Ending

1. Dad took his fishing pole out of the garage, then… — **c** he went fishing.
2. Mom sent Maria to the grocery store so… — **a** she could buy milk and eggs.
3. Amy filled the bathtub with warm water, then… — **c** she took a bubble bath.
4. Lee's dog, Rex, was hungry, so… — **c** he sat by his food dish and barked.

B

Center Mat B: Predict the Ending

5. When the wind blew, … — **a** the kite flew up into the sky.
6. The campers built a campfire, then… — **a** they roasted marshmallows.
7. Millie took out bread and peanut butter, then… — **c** she made a sandwich for lunch.
8. Bob got on an airplane, then… — **b** he buckled his seat belt.

C

Center Mat C: Predict the Ending

9. The light turned green, so… — **b** the driver drove away.
10. His bike had a flat tire, so… — **c** the man fixed the flat tire.
11. The cat curled up on a chair, and… — **a** she took a nap.
12. The hen sat on her nest until… — **c** the chicks hatched out of the eggs.

Center Mat A

Predict the Ending

1. Dad took his fishing pole out of the garage, then…

2. Mom sent Maria to the grocery store so…

3. Amy filled the bathtub with warm water, then…

4. Lee's dog, Rex, was hungry, so…

Center Mat B

Predict the Ending

5 When the wind blew, …

6 The campers built a campfire, then…

7 Millie took out bread and peanut butter, then…

8 Bob got on an airplane, then…

Center Mat C

Predict the Ending

9 The light turned green, so…

10 His bike had a flat tire, so…

11 The cat curled up on a chair, and…

12 The hen sat on her nest until…

a	b	c
he went to work.	he went for a walk.	he went fishing.
she could buy milk and eggs.	she could pick up a new puppy.	she could play with her new friends.
she ate a snack.	she made her bed.	she took a bubble bath.
he ran around the backyard.	he took a nap on his bed.	he sat by his food dish and barked.
the kite flew up into the sky.	the kite never moved off the ground.	the kite began to sing.
they roasted marshmallows.	they watched TV.	they hiked over the mountain.

Predict the Ending
Take It to Your Seat Centers
Reading & Language
EMC 2842 • © Evan-Moor Corp.

Predict the Ending
Take It to Your Seat Centers
Reading & Language
EMC 2842 • © Evan-Moor Corp.

Predict the Ending
Take It to Your Seat Centers
Reading & Language
EMC 2842 • © Evan-Moor Corp.

Predict the Ending
Take It to Your Seat Centers
Reading & Language
EMC 2842 • © Evan-Moor Corp.

Predict the Ending
Take It to Your Seat Centers
Reading & Language
EMC 2842 • © Evan-Moor Corp.

Predict the Ending
Take It to Your Seat Centers
Reading & Language
EMC 2842 • © Evan-Moor Corp.

Predict the Ending
Take It to Your Seat Centers
Reading & Language
EMC 2842 • © Evan-Moor Corp.

Predict the Ending
Take It to Your Seat Centers
Reading & Language
EMC 2842 • © Evan-Moor Corp.

Predict the Ending
Take It to Your Seat Centers
Reading & Language
EMC 2842 • © Evan-Moor Corp.

Predict the Ending
Take It to Your Seat Centers
Reading & Language
EMC 2842 • © Evan-Moor Corp.

Predict the Ending
Take It to Your Seat Centers
Reading & Language
EMC 2842 • © Evan-Moor Corp.

Predict the Ending
Take It to Your Seat Centers
Reading & Language
EMC 2842 • © Evan-Moor Corp.

Predict the Ending
Take It to Your Seat Centers
Reading & Language
EMC 2842 • © Evan-Moor Corp.

Predict the Ending
Take It to Your Seat Centers
Reading & Language
EMC 2842 • © Evan-Moor Corp.

Predict the Ending
Take It to Your Seat Centers
Reading & Language
EMC 2842 • © Evan-Moor Corp.

Predict the Ending
Take It to Your Seat Centers
Reading & Language
EMC 2842 • © Evan-Moor Corp.

Predict the Ending
Take It to Your Seat Centers
Reading & Language
EMC 2842 • © Evan-Moor Corp.

Predict the Ending
Take It to Your Seat Centers
Reading & Language
EMC 2842 • © Evan-Moor Corp.